Administering
Foreign-Worker
Programs

Administering Foreign-Worker Programs

Lessons from Europe

Mark J. Miller
University of Delaware
Philip L. Martin
University of California, Davis

LexingtonBooks
D.C. Heath and Company
Lexington, Massachusetts
Toronto

Library of Congress Cataloging in Publication Data

Miller, Mark J.
  Administering foreign-worker programs.

  Includes bibliographical references and index.
  1. Alien labor—Europe.   2. Europe—Emigration and immigration.
3. Europe—Foreign population.
I. Martin, Philip L., 1949-   . II. Title.
HD8378.5.A2M539   331.6′2   81-47994
ISBN 0-669-05227-2   AACR2

Published simultaneously in Canada

Printed in the United States of America

International Standard Book Number: 0-669-05227-2

Library of Congress Catalog Card Number: 81-47994

To Europe's Foreign Workers

For the ones are in the darkness
and the others in the light,
one can see those in the light,
those in darkness no one sees.

—The Threepenny Opera

Contents

Contents

List of Tables

Acknowledgments

A U.S. Department of Labor contract to examine the administration of foreign-worker programs in Europe provided the original impetus for this book. A German Marshall Fund of the United States grant enabled us to conduct research on the topic in Western Europe. We are grateful for the support of both organizations.

A warm note of appreciation is due to individuals in the United States and Western Europe who aided in our research. In France, André Lebon of the Labor Ministry, Barthélemy Capmal of the National Immigration Office, Denis Jacquot of the Confédération Française Democratique du Travail (CFDT), and Michel Anselme were particularly helpful. As always, the librarians of the Centre d'information et d'études sur les migrations and Catherine Wihtol de Wenden-Didier provided indispensable assistance.

In Switzerland, W.R. Böhning, J.H. Lasserre-Bigorry, and Italo Musillo of the ILO facilitated the gathering of information on regional and international instruments relevant to migrant workers. Renée Rideau of the International Catholic Migration Commission and Hermann Heinzmann of the Federal Commission for the Aliens Problem generously provided materials on Swiss policy administration.

In the Federal Republic of Germany, Elmer Hönekopp and Hans Ullman made very useful background material available to us. Werner Sengenberger, Hermann Korte, and Sigfried Mueller patiently explained the German guest-worker system. Hannelore Koehler of the German Information Center in New York also contributed to the gathering of materials on German guest-worker policy.

Marion Houstoun of the International Labor Affairs Bureau of the Department of Labor deserves special thanks. She recognized the importance of the European experience and assisted us in many ways. Ellen Seghal, Elizabeth Midgley, and David North provided indispensable encouragement. We would also like to thank Beverly Miller for her excellent copyediting and Marjorie Glazer of Lexington Books for her fine work in producing this book.

We remain fully responsible for the contents, which do not necessarily reflect the official viewpoint of any national or international governmental agency.

Introduction

Illegal immigration, employer complaints of labor shortages despite persisting unemployment, slow labor-force growth, and pressure to make the U.S. labor market a safety valve for unemployment abroad prompt calls for a guest-worker program. By definition, guest-worker policy would admit aliens to work in the United States on a nonimmigrant or temporary basis. Southwestern agri-businessmen and Congressmen, some immigration policy specialists and several key members of the Reagan administration have been the most visible guest-worker policy advocates. Such a migrant-worker plan could admit 300,000 to 800,000 foreign nationals annually for employment in the United States. After several months or years, the workers would be expected to return to their home countries.

Although the United States has had relatively little experience with nonimmigrant guest-workers, Western European nations recruited millions of temporary foreign workers between 1960 and 1973. These foreign workers came to comprise 10 percent of the work forces of France and Germany and 25 percent of all Swiss workers.

This book examines six major administrative issues common to foreign-worker programs in advanced industrial democracies:

1. Determining the need for foreign workers at employer, industry, regional, and national levels.
2. Determining the legal basis for admitting foreign labor.
3. Developing procedures for recruiting, screening, and transporting migrant workers.
4. Establishing and protecting employment-related rights for foreign workers.
5. Establishing and protecting the nonemployment-related rights of migrant workers and their dependents.
6. Planning for the return or integration of foreign workers and their dependents.

European responses to these policy issues are described and analyzed in view of a proposed U.S. guest-worker program.

Western European recourse to foreign workers fundamentally was a response to perceived temporary manpower shortages in the postwar period of economic expansion. Such shortages proved to be persistent, however, especially in manual-labor jobs in manufacturing, construction, and services. Even with the recession in the mid-1970s and resultant high levels of unemployment, European employers feared that unemployed nationals would not take the menial jobs often held by foreign workers. The number of foreign job holders declined after 1973, but foreign populations remained steady or grew slightly due to the birth or migration of dependents. The foreign workers, originally thought to be a temporary phenomenon, had become a permanent, resident population by the mid-1970s. Neither the number nor the permanence of these postwar European migrations was anticipated.

Expectations that unemployment would force migrant workers to return home proved to be shortsighted. In 1973 some 7 million foreign workers were employed in Western Europe. Such a massive foreign work force concentrated in blue-collar jobs had become a structural element of Western European labor markets. Considerable economic dislocation would have resulted if labor-recruiting countries forced the migrants to leave. Hence, relatively few foreign workers have been constrained to leave through outright withdrawal of work and residency permits. However, European governments favor voluntary foreign-worker repatriation, and France even provides cash bonuses to induce returns.

Over the years, Western European economies became dependent on foreign workers to fill manual-labor posts, which increasingly their own nationals shunned. Recourse to foreign labor seems to have encouraged the development of labor-market segments. The least desirable jobs in the lowest segments are largely held by foreign workers. However, with time and the easing of permit restrictions, foreign workers are moving into skilled and sometimes nonmanual job categories. It remains to be seen whether high rates of unemployment will lower the barriers that keep Western Europeans from accepting the kinds of jobs now associated with foreign workers. A French program designed to attract French workers to manual-labor jobs now usually held by aliens has met with mixed results.

The phenomenon of foreign-worker concentration in certain blue-collar jobs stems in part from administrative procedures. Foreign workers, except European Economic Community (EEC) nationals, initially were authorized to work for a specific employer. During periods of manpower shortages in the 1960s, employer recourse to foreign labor generally received routine approval. Labor-market considerations were the primary determinants of need for foreign labor, although restrictions on the types of work foreigners could accept and the location of their employment continued after they became free to switch employers. During the 1960s, there seems to have been little direct competition between foreigners and nationals for jobs. As restrictions on foreign workers were eased and the general economic picture clouded, however, displacement of native workers by foreign labor became an issue.

Postwar labor migration to Western Europe has been authorized by a series of bilateral and multilateral agreements. The varying legal statuses accorded various foreign-worker nationality groups under these agreements gradually have been homogenized as employment and residency restrictions have been eased, although important gradations of privileges remain concerning EEC, non-EEC, and seasonal foreign workers. International organizations, such as the International Labour Office and the Council of Europe, monitor treatment of foreign workers and have encouraged labor-importing countries to grant to all foreign workers the rights afforded to EEC nationals. Nonetheless, Western European hosts of foreign labor retain final discretion in policy matters, and, in several instances, their policies toward foreign workers have resulted in strained relations with the labor exporting countries.

Foreign-worker recruitment in the 1960s generally was organized under Western European governmental auspices in conjunction with the governments of emigrant-sending countries. However, the Swiss did permit direct employer-foreign-worker contracting subject to approval by Swiss authorities. In most cases, aspiring foreign workers were screened for employment skills and medical purposes, required to sign translated work contracts, and given orientation before being transported to Western Europe. Despite these established procedures, a significant number of foreign workers, especially in the French case, entered labor-recruiting countries and took employment illegally. During the decade of general manpower shortages in the 1960s, several governments, notably France and Belgium, legalized these illegal aliens post facto. In the 1970s these periodic adjustment-of-status amnesties were largely stopped, contributing to a growing illegal-alien problem.

While foreign-worker legal statuses differ, virtually all now have extensive employment-related and social rights. Except for seasonal workers in Switzerland and, in some instances, in France, dependents can join foreign workers after one year. Foreign workers can join unions, are protected by labor laws and social security systems, have access to most social services, and in most cases are legally protected from discrimination in housing, education, and other areas. Despite these extensive formal protections, however, a pattern of poor housing, educational problems among migrant children, administrative neglect, and socioeconomic discrimination is apparent. Resentment by nationals over social expenditures for foreign workers and their dependents, coupled with increasingly salient integration problems, contributed to decisions made in 1973-1974 to stop foreign-worker recruitment. The recruitment bans, which do not concern EEC and seasonal workers, have only infrequently been lifted in special cases since 1973-1974, and there is little chance that recruitment will be renewed in the future.

At present, foreign workers and their dependents are one of Western Europe's significant, long-term socioeconomic and political problems. Foreign workers themselves, their homeland governments, and Western European authorities are all, in various ways, locked into a dilemma over /

whether to integrate the migrants or encourage them to depart. Labor emigration has not fundamentally altered poor economic circumstances in the homelands. Because migrants, their home governments, and the host countries are ambivalent toward integration, neither return nor satisfactory integration has been accomplished.

Foreign workers helped spur noninflationary economic growth in Western Europe for two decades. European inability to resolve the integration-versus-return conundrum satisfactorily, however, has prompted a sociopolitical malaise. Labor-recruiting countries have learned that guest-worker programs are far easier to start than stop.

If the United States decides to expand its nonimmigrant work force, it would not necessarily replicate the Western European experience with foreign labor. Indeed, one purpose of this study is to indicate the United States can avoid making the same mistakes as Western Europe has in the event of a nonimmigrant labor-program expansion. Furthermore, important socioeconomic and politicocultural differences would distinguish an expanded U.S. temporary-worker program from the Western European case. The lessons or comparative insights to be derived from the Western European experience, nonetheless, have both policy planning and practical administrative significance. Such insights contribute to a rational calculation of likely benefits and drawbacks resulting from expanded temporary foreign-worker policy, and they point to the key administrative decisions that must be made if nonimmigrant labor policy is to be expanded in the United States.

Reflection on Western Europe's foreign-worker experience warns against misplaced confidence in foreign-worker policy as a means of ameliorating the U.S. illegal-alien problem. Foreign-worker policy may be incompatible with democratic ideals and foster long-term sociopolitical problems for reasons of short-term economic or diplomatic expediency. Hence, there is a need for cross-national public-policy learning in this salient area for advanced industrial democracies.

**Administering
Foreign-Worker
Programs**

Immigration Policy: Not Only an American Issue

Immigration and Naturalization Service (INS) apprehensions of aliens illegally in the United States have increased almost tenfold since 1970. The continuing increase in apprehensions, the effects that nonapprehended aliens have had, and few prospects for a "natural" cessation of this alien influx (due to the diminishment of factors encouraging illegal migration such as high levels of unemployment in the third world) have prompted a variety of federal efforts to study and revise immigration laws and policies.[1] Both domestic and international considerations have made a large-scale temporary foreign-worker or guest-worker program that could admit 300,000 to 800,000 nonimmigrant workers annually a widely discussed policy option. President Ronald Reagan reportedly made a great deal of progress toward initiating a guest-worker program with Mexico in June 1981.[2] Most advocates maintain that a nonimmigrant-labor program of this kind could curb illegal migration, protect the human and labor rights of undocumented migrants, fill vacancies in the lower tiers of the labor market, help relieve wage-induced inflationary pressures, improve bilateral relations now strained by the illegal-alien situation, and promote economic development in labor-surplus nations.

Currently the United States issues some 30,000 visas annually to nonimmigrant workers. Some 9,000 to 12,000 temporary work visas go to unskilled foreigners for agricultural employment.[3] Commonly referred to as the H-2 program, this exception to the legal ban on nonimmigrant labor is authorized under the H(ii) section of the Immigration and Naturalization Act of 1952, as amended. H-2 entrants are temporary workers required by law to work only in agricultural or nonagricultural jobs of a temporary character.

Prior to the refusal of the Eighty-eighth Congress to renew public law 78 in 1964, much more extensive employer recourse to temporary foreign labor was permitted.[4] Between 1942 and 1964 almost 5 million Mexican nationals were admitted under the auspices of what came to be known as the *bracero* program. These braceros ("strong-armed ones") were employed primarily in southwestern agriculture, although some employment outside of the Southwest and in nonagricultural jobs also was permitted. Despite its long duration, the bracero program was begun as a temporary measure to relieve wartime manpower shortages. Hence, the H-2 program and the bracero program are anomalies in the U.S. tradition of welcoming immigrant settlers.

1

In contrast to the United States, Western European governments recruited some 30 million foreign workers between 1960 and 1973. At its peak in the early 1970s, the nine European Economic Community (EEC) nations (excluding Italy and Ireland) together with Austria, Switzerland, and Sweden were admitting more than a million alien workers and their dependents annually. Foreign workers generally constituted between 6 and 10 percent of host-country work forces but represented almost 30 percent in Switzerland.

Recruitment of foreign workers, with a few exceptions, was stopped by 1974 because of the oil crisis, unemployment, and sociopolitical tensions over foreign workers and their dependents. Despite the continuation of these recruitment bans, at least 5 million foreign workers and an additional 8 million dependents now reside in Western European host societies, which have a population of roughly 220 million.

The Rationale for Comparison

Western European countries, with the limited exceptions of France and Belgium, do not have immigrant-welcoming traditions. Their foreign.manpower policies were not based on the assumption that migration should eventuate in citizenship. Instead Western European governments generally conceived of postwar labor migration as temporary in nature. Even now, when millions of foreign workers and their dependents have become de facto permanent residents, barriers to naturalization remain, and relatively few foreign workers become citizens, except in France.

This expectation of temporary migration was shared by the labor-sending countries and the migrant workers themselves. This assumption demarcates postwar labor migration to Western Europe from the United States' tradition of immigration. Lawful international migration to the United States is assumed to be motivated by a desire to acquire U.S. citizenship. If the United States does begin a large-scale temporary-worker program, it would be broadly comparable with postwar Western European foreign-worker policies because it would diverge from the immigrant-welcoming tradition of the United States.

The United States can learn much from the Western European experience with large-scale foreign-worker programs, in both a policy-planning and a practical administrative sense. Although labor markets and administrative structures differ both within Western Europe and with the United States, all regulated international labor flows have common features requiring fundamental policy decisions. These features can be illustrated by the following questions:

1. How should the need for foreign workers be determined? What labor-market tests must be satisfied before alien workers can be admitted? How should a work-permit system function?

2. How should foreign workers be admitted? What will be the international and domestic legal basis for admission? Should all foreign workers have similar rights and obligations, or should various nationalities be admitted on different terms?

3. What procedures should be used to recruit and employ foreign workers? What should be the roles of host and sending governments, employers, and unions in the recruitment, screening, transportation, and employment of foreign workers?

4. What employment-related entitlements should foreign workers have? Will they be restricted to certain jobs or areas? Will they have access to language and occupational training? Will housing be provided by employers? Who will administer and enforce these entitlements and restrictions?

5. What sociopolitical entitlements ought foreign workers to have? Will foreign workers be allowed to bring their families? Will they have access to social services? Can they vote or run for political office?

6. Should foreign-worker repatriation be mandatory, or should provision be made to integrate foreign workers and their dependents? How is repatriation to be enforced or encouraged? Will labor-sending countries accept forced repatriation of their nationals? Will labor-sending countries cooperate in preparing and encouraging return? Should foreign workers have access to immigrant and eventual citizenship status? How will work and residence permit violators and illegal aliens be treated?

Foreign-worker policy in any advanced industrial democracy is largely shaped by responses to these questions. The underlying sociocultural, economic, and political similarities between Western democracies facilitates comparative analysis. However, several comparative caveats are in order.

Contextual Dissimilarities

At the time of Western European foreign-worker policy formation, economic conditions and the international environment differed sharply from the current policy context in the United States. In particular, Western European foreign-labor policies developed in an era of extraordinary economic expansion that led to labor scarcities. In the late 1950s and throughout the 1960s (except 1966-1967), Western European unemployment rates hovered around zero. With the limited exceptions of France and Belgium, Western European nations also had (and continue to have) comparatively little legal immigration and small illegal-alien populations, although this latter group probably has increased in recent years. Hence, Western Europeans had far more of a tabula rasa when formulating foreign-worker policy than is the case with the United States. Guest-worker policy in the United States would have to be formulated with a view toward the reality of a large, resident illegal-alien population, a factor complicating the implementation of guest-worker policy in the United States when compared to Western Europe of the 1960s.

In addition, Western European institutions and administrative structures already in place facilitated the management of foreign workers. That is, European governments have more controls over residents and labor-market entry than in the United States. The long-standing obligation in these countries to provide proof of identity at the request of authorities has facilitated the monitoring of foreign workers. Similarly, the tendency to funnel all job vacancies and applicants through nationwide, government-operated employment exchanges has minimized the need for elaborate local tests of domestic worker availability.

Despite these seemingly propitious contextual factors, Western European foreign-worker policies have evolved from ad hoc rules and piecemeal decision making. The present European dilemma over foreign workers stems in large part from the unplanned or unanticipated permanent addition of millions of foreign workers and their dependents to Western European societies. The initial lesson Western Europe provides for U.S. policymakers is the need to take a comprehensive view of foreign-worker policy, anticipating and resolving issues requiring decisions before launching a large-scale program.

The nature of the Western European response to the six groups of questions pertaining to foreign-worker policy provides the organizational structure of this book. First, however, an overview of the postwar evolution of Western European (especially French, German, and Swiss) foreign-worker policies is undertaken in chapter 2. Since three-quarters of Western Europe's foreign workers are located in France, Switzerland, and the Federal Republic of Germany, the essence of the Western European foreign-worker experience can be conveyed by concentrating on these three examples.

Chapter 3 examines Western European labor-market tests or the process of establishing individual employer, industry, regional, or national need for foreign labor. Chapter 4 surveys the legal basis underpinning labor flows to Western Europe, reviewing germane EEC treaties, bilateral labor agreements, and the role of international guidelines. Chapter 5 analyzes the administrative procedures used to bring foreign workers to jobs in Europe, and chapters 6 and 7 focus on migrant worker employment-related and sociopolitical rights as well as their enforcement.

An assessment of postwar European foreign-worker policies and the prospects for resolving the European dilemma over foreign workers is made in chapter 8. A survey of the effects of labor emigrations on the emigrant-sending countries of the Mediterranean basin in chapter 9 completes the substantive part of the study. Chapter 10 assesses the Western European foreign-worker experience in light of advocacy of an expanded U.S. non-immigrant-labor policy. The appendixes summarize foreign-worker employment-related and sociopolitical entitlements in Western Europe, International Labour Organization conventions concerning migrant workers, certification and work permit procedures, and the evolution of EEC membership.

Notes

1. See Select Commission on Immigration and Refugee Policy, *U.S. Immigration Policy and the National Interest* (Washington, D.C.: U.S. Government Printing Office, 1981).

2. Howell Rains, "Reagan Advised to Admit Mexicans as Guest Workers," *New York Times*, July 2, 1981.

3. See Congressional Research Service, *Temporary Worker Programs: Background and Issues* (Washington, D.C.: U.S. Government Printing Office, 1980), pp. 58-80.

4. Public law 78 had authorized bracero employment since 1951. Ellis W. Hawley, "The Politics of the Mexican Labor Issue, 1950-1965" in George C. Kiser and Martha Woody Kiser, *Mexican Workers in the United States* (Albuquerque: University of New Mexico Press, 1979).

2

The Postwar Evolution of Western European Foreign-Worker Policies

Western Europe was the source of massive out-migration in the eighteenth and nineteenth centuries. By 1900, however, influxes of Polish workers to the Ruhr area of Germany and of Italian emigrant workers to Switzerland and eastern France had occurred. Significantly, the ambiguous Swiss term *Überfremdung*, connoting fear of loss of identity due to the presence of large numbers of foreigners, came into usage prior to World War I. In the interwar period, labor flows, bolstered by political refugees, increased. By 1932, 7 percent of the total French population was foreign, prompting the enactment of laws designed to protect the native work force.[1] A French government-backed repatriation drive during the Great Depression succeeded in reducing the foreign population by almost 500,000.[2] The major legacy of the interwar period for postwar migration policy was the need for a repatriation policy if economic depression and high rates of unemployment recurred. This generalized fear throughout Western Europe cautioned against the permanent admission of foreign workers in the immediate postwar period.

Policy Formation

The postwar Western European phenomenon of massive recourse to foreign labor occurred first in Switzerland. Unlike its neighbors, Swiss industry emerged from World War II unscathed. During the period of postwar reconstruction, the Swiss economy experienced a boom in demand for manufactured goods, which led to a long period of economic expansion. The rapid rate of Swiss economic expansion led to acute manpower shortages, especially in manual labor, which gave rise to employer demands for foreign labor. In 1948, the government acquiesced to these demands, and a bilateral labor treaty was signed with Italy. The hallmark of Swiss foreign-labor policy since its inception has been that foreign workers comprise a complementary work force providing manpower elasticity. Swiss officials never have considered their insular mountain confederacy to be a classic immigration country.[3]

Massive recourse to foreign labor did not occur elsewhere in Western Europe until the early 1960s. The Federal Republic of Germany experienced a high rate of unemployment in the immediate postwar years. When the nascent

Wirtschaftswüder (economic miracle) increased manpower demands, the steady influx of ethnic German refugees from Eastern Europe largely filled the supply-demand gap. However, the origins of postwar German foreign-worker policy can be traced back to 1955 when several thousand Italian farmworkers were granted temporary work permits. Massive foreign-labor emigration to Germany began only after the construction of the Berlin wall in 1961 stopped the influx of ethnic German refugees from Eastern Europe.

The major comparative difference between France and its eastern neighbors in the realm of migration policy is that France long has considered itself an immigrant-welcoming country. The French birthrate plummeted in the nineteenth century, precursing the low birthrates now characteristic of postindustrial societies. The premature decline in the French birthrate combined with France's frightful war losses (2.4 million dead and maimed in World War I out of a population of 39 million) prompted concern over what the French refer to as their demographic insufficiency. In the aftermath of World War II, several French governmental commissions advocated large-scale permanent immigration as part of a broader population-growth strategy. Neighboring Belgium also favored permanent immigration for demographic-economic purposes during the 1950s and 1960s.[4] Hence France and Belgium constitute limited exceptions to the general postwar policy assumption of temporary labor migration.

Despite repeated calls for large-scale immigration, especially by Gaullists, French postwar immigration goals were not achieved. The opposition of the major French trade union and the French Communist party (PCF) to governmental immigration policy (once PCF participation in French government ended in 1947) did little to impede policy implementation. Rather, the outbreak of the Algerian war in 1954, and, to a lesser extent, administrative ineptitude thwarted plans for massive immigration.[5]

The French hoped to attract easily assimilable immigrants from Catholic Italy and Spain but ended up instead with a large, nonpermanent foreign-worker population regarded as difficult to assimilate. In the effort to stifle the Algerian nationalist movement, Algerian Muslims were conceded additional rights in 1947, including the right to come to mainland France and take a job. This set in motion a stream of Algerian labor emigration with legal priority over prospective Italian or Spanish migrants. The opening up of mainland France to Algerian workers was a major reason why far fewer Italians and Spaniards came than planned. The French governmental body established to promote and administer immigration policy, the National Immigration Office (ONI), experienced bureaucratic problems, which further hampered recruitment of Spanish and Italian immigrants. The tempo of Algerian labor migration to France picked up when guerrilla warfare broke out, and, by the 1962 victory of the Algerian nationalists, over 300,000 Algerians were living in mainland France.[6] Under the terms of the Evian peace treaty, Algerians living in France could choose French citizenship, but most chose Algerian citizenship and, under the terms of the treaty, could stay on in France as privileged foreign residents.

Two notable multilateral treaties signed in the 1950s contained important free-movement-of-labor provisions for citizens of member states. In 1954, Sweden, Norway, Denmark, and Finland formed the Common Nordic Labor Market. Their agreement allowed nationals of fellow signatory states to take work without special work permits, and it provided for employment service cooperation.[7] More important, though, was the signing of the Treaty of Rome in 1957, which created the European Economic Community (EEC). The six original member states—France, the Federal Republic of Germany, Italy, Belgium, Luxembourg, and the Netherlands—agreed to implement free movement of labor in stages over a ten-year transition period, a provision that had a political and economic rationale. While intracommunity labor transfers were assumed to be mutually beneficial to labor exporter and receiving states, EEC workers were seen as precursors of the European citizen envisioned for the future. Freedom of labor movement was seen as a logical step in the direction of eventual political integration. Hence migration between member states could be on a permanent basis. The major labor surplus area within the EEC was southern Italy, and consequently Italians made up the bulk of early intracommunity migrants. Nevertheless by 1959 fewer than half of the foreign workers within the EEC were so-called community workers (nationals from EEC member states), and by 1978, community workers represented only a quarter of the foreign work force in the original six EEC members.[8]

The prolonged, eventually European-wide, economic boom of the late 1950s and early 1960s created labor demand that could not be satisfied by southern Italy alone. Increasingly foreign workers from physically and culturally more distant societies were recruited. Bilateral labor agreements were signed between Germany and Greece, Spain, Turkey, Morocco, Portugal, and Tunisia between 1960 and 1965. In 1968, Germany signed a similar agreement with Yugoslavia. Non-EEC member Switzerland signed a bilateral labor agreement with Spain in 1964 while renegotiating its labor treaty with Italy in that same year. France signed agreements with Spain in 1961, Morocco and Tunisia in 1963, Turkey in 1965, and Portugal in 1971 while continuing to permit Algerian labor emigration on the basis of Franco-Algerian agreements reached in 1964 and 1968.

Germany, like Switzerland, does not consider itself to be an immigration country. Its massive recruitment of foreign workers was predicated on the corollary assumptions that the need for foreign labor would be ephemeral and that the foreign workers themselves would not stay on permanently. Significantly, the German term for them, *Gastarbeiter* ("guest worker"), conveys the idea that the alien workers were expected to return home.

Despite France's official policy of welcoming immigration, the surge in migration to France, Switzerland, and Germany in the late 1950s and early 1960s fundamentally was a response to labor shortages. Most migrants to France during the 1960s did not come as immigrants under the auspices of the ONI but rather as temporary workers who would receive legal status after technically illegal entry. The circumstances of postwar labor migration to France, then, were quite similar to the nonimmigrant-welcoming German and Swiss cases. Since the 1950s, France has had a dualistic migratory policy, welcoming the naturalization of "assimilable" foreign workers (Italian, Spanish, and Portuguese) and permitting but not welcoming the naturalization of "unassimilable" foreigners (Arabs, Turks, and more recently black Africans).[9]

As France's attachments to its former colonies have waned and integration and unemployment problems have increased, the French government has slowly but steadily reoriented its migratory policies toward the German-Swiss model. This long-term trend crystallized in the late 1970s when the French government offered cash bonuses to repatriating migrants and the French minister in charge of foreign-worker affairs declared that "what beforehand was an immigration country will become an emigration country."[10]

Policy Stabilization

Table 2-1 records the tremendous growth of the French, German, and Swiss foreign populations in the 1960s and early 1970s and is indicative of European-wide trends. The foreign population of Western Europe peaked in 1973-1974 at 14 million, excluding illegal aliens. In the 1973-1975 period, all of the major labor-recruiting countries stopped foreign-worker recruitment. Dependents, however, were permitted to continue joining breadwinners in Western Europe. EEC nationals and seasonal workers in France and Switzerland were not directly affected by the recruitment bans.

Explanations for the recruitment halts vary. The oil crisis and its expected resultant unemployment usually were cited in official pronouncements, but growing concern over integration problems and the realization that many foreign workers would not voluntarily depart as expected were also cited frequently.

Since the recruitment halts, foreign populations have not decreased despite the fact that some 2 million foreigners lost the jobs they held in 1973-1974.[11] The continuing inflow of dependents and the relatively high birthrate of foreign workers have offset the exodus of unemployed workers. Relatively few unemployed foreigners were forced to return home through denial of work-permit renewal. One important result, then, of the recruit-

Table 2-1

Foreign Population in France, Switzerland, and the Federal Republic of Germany for Selected Years, 1946-1980

Year	Switzerland		France		Federal Republic Germany	
1946			1,743,619	(4.35)		
1950	285,446	(6.05)				
1951					485,763	(0.99)
1954			1,766,100	(4.09)		
1955					484,819	(0.92)
1958			1,621,075	(3.60)		
1960	469,924	(10.50)	1,633,410	(3.56)		
1961					686,160	(1.22)
1965	810,243	(13.47)	2,683,490	(5.48)		
1968	933,142	(15.21)			2,318,100	(3.96)
1970	982,887	(15.68)	3,393,457	(6.65)	2,976,500	(4.90)
1972			3,775,804	(7.21)	3,438,700	(5.58)
1974	1,064,529	(16.52)	4,138,312	(7.70)	4,127,400	(6.65)
1975	1,012,710				4,089,000	(6.59)
1976	985,599	(15.19)				
1977	932,743		4,236,944	(8.00)		
1979	883,837		4,127,317	(7.69)	4,253,000	(6.92)
1980	885,178[a]		4,147,978	(8.00)	4,453,300	(7.00)

Sources: Ray Rist, *Guestworkers in Germany,* (New York: Praeger, 1978), pp. 8-11; Ministère du travail et de la participation, *Le dossier de l'immigration,* November 1978, p. 2; German Information Center, *The Week in Germany,* June 13, 1980, p. 6; *Le Monde,* January 26, 1981, p. 10, "Bestand der ausländischen Arbeitskrafte, Ende August 1980;" *Volkswirtschaft,* October, 1980, pp. 663-667.

Note: Figures in parentheses are percentage of total population.

[a]August, 1980 total.

ment bans has been a decline in the migrant work force but an increase in the inactive foreign population. There now are some 5 million working foreigners and an additional 8 million dependents of foreign workers. Table 2-2 compares the activity rates of foreign and citizen populations in France, Switzerland, and Germany in 1976.

The decade of the 1970s witnessed the emergence of immigrant or foreign-labor-related sociopolitical questions as salient issues across Western Europe. The earliest and perhaps best-known protest movement against foreign-labor policy developed in Switzerland in the early 1960s. Protests against *Überfremdung* led to a series of closely contested referendums, which, if they had passed, would have forced the Swiss government to reduce the foreign population drastically. Although the referendums were defeated, the antiforeign-worker protest movement did prompt the Swiss government to stabilize and then gradually reduce alien employment.

Table 2-2
Foreign Workers as a Percentage of the Economically Active
Population, 1976

	France	Federal Republic of Germany	Switzerland
Total population	52,841,746	61,542,000	6,269,783
Total work force	22,133,600	26,696,000	2,995,777
Overall labor force participation (percent)	41.9	43.4	47.8
Foreign population	4,125,000	4,090,000	1,013,000
Foreign workers	1,900,000	2,171,000	533,000[a]
Migrant activity rate (percent)	46.1	53.1	55.6
Foreign share of total population (percent)	7.8	6.6	15.8
Foreign share of workforce (percent)	10.9	9.7	19.8

Sources: *Sozialpolitische Umschau,* no. 14 (January 27, 1978):2; International Labor Organization, *1977 Yearbook of Labor Statistics* (Geneva: ILO, 1978), pp. 39, 40, and 45.

[a]Does not include seasonal or frontier workers.

Great Britain also experienced unrest over its immigration policy in the 1960s, which eventually led to a curtailment of new immigration through progressively more restrictive legislation. Table 2-3 indicates, however, that so-called "coloured" immigration to Britain was not curtailed, largely because of the entry of dependents of immigrants resident in Great Britain prior to passage of the Commonwealth Immigrant Act of 1962. Since controls were put on immigration and work vouchers required before entering the country, new immigration of colored workers has dwindled (table 2-4). Unlike the foreign-worker situation prevailing on the Continent, Commonwealth subjects and citizens of the Irish Republic moving to Great Britain automatically become citizens and are extended voting rights. Despite the cutback, immigration and racial policies remain important issues in Great Britain, as indicated by Prime Minister Margaret Thatcher's appeal to anti-immigrant sentiments in the 1979 parliamentary elections and the July 1981 clashes involving immigrants and the police.[12]

Integration problems that are similar to those of the Swiss and British have become apparent in other European settings. In the Netherlands, which has a colonial heritage like that of France, Belgium, and Great Britain, the arrival of Dutch subjects from the West Indies, Surinam, and the Far East coupled with large-scale recruitment of Turkish and Moroccan workers sparked racial incidents in 1971.[13] And in Sweden and Norway, unease over workers gave rise to discrimination and, albeit infrequently, to racial incidents in the 1970s.[14]

Table 2-3
Coloured Immigration to Great Britain, 1955-1976

1955	35,299
1956	37,450
1957	34,800
1958	25,900
1959	27,400
1960	58,050
1961	115,150
1962	88,983
1963	56,971
1964	52,840
1965	53,650
1966	46,602
1967	57,648
1968	56,203
1969	44,503
1970	37,883
1971	44,261
1972	68,519
1973	32,247
1874	42,531
1975	53,265
1976	55,000[a]

Sources: Adapted from Gary P. Freeman, *Immigrant Labor and Racial Conflict in Industrial Societies* (Princeton: Princeton University Press, 1978), p. 23, and Donley T. Studlar, "Great Britain," in *International Labor Migration in Europe*, R.E. Krahe (New Yorker: Praeger, 1979), p. 94.
[a]Provisional figure.

Due to their Common Nordic Labor Market status, Norway, Sweden, and Denmark have foreign-labor situations dissimilar in several important respects from those of Western European host countries to the south. In Sweden, for example, 46 percent of all foreign workers in 1977 were from

Table 2-4
Coloured Ministry of Labour Voucher Holders Admitted, 1962-1972

1962	2,637
1963	23,969
1964	9,759
1965	9,301
1966	3,782
1967	3,559
1968	1,544
1969	2,197
1970	1,494
1971	1,040
1972	348

Source: Gary P. Freeman, *Immigrant Labor and Racial Conflict in Industrial Societies*, (Princeton: Princeton University Press, 1978), p. 24.

neighboring Finland.[15] Similarly the Danes and Norwegians have high percentages of Nordic Labor Market workers who do not encounter adaptation and cultural barriers comparable to those encountered by Turks in Germany, Mahgrebians in France, and Sicilians in Switzerland. Nonetheless, when Norway announced its decision to ban foreign-worker recruitment in 1975 (not applicable to Common Nordic Labor Market workers), it cited integration problems encountered with its small foreign-worker community from the Mediterranean basin.

Table 2-5 provides an overview of the foreign-worker populations of major Western European host countries by nationality in 1977. Italian workers still play minor roles vis-à-vis non-EEC workers in France and Germany despite the fact that Italian workers were not affected by the French and German labor recruitment bans. The intended effect of these bans has been partially frustrated by foreign-worker dependents' entering the job market. In Germany also, it was estimated that 200,000 jobs would have to be found between 1975 and 1980 for the children of guest workers.[16]

Problems and Prospects for the 1980s

Currently the second-generation problem dominates public discussion of foreign-worker policy. Millions of foreign-worker children have grown up as noncitizens in Western Europe or recently have joined their parents there. Second-generation educational, social, and cultural problems are seen by many experts as a "potential social time bomb."[17] Most such children now entering the job market are qualified only for blue-collar jobs despite having higher socioeconomic aspirations than their parents. A young Algerian's chances of finding any work at all, for example, are significantly dimmer than those of a young French national in periods of high unemployment.

For general economic reasons and because of the problems of integration, no Western European country currently contemplates resumption of foreign-worker recruitment. Instead a great deal of attention in recent years has been devoted to the formulation of repatriation strategies. Thus far, Western European governments have shunned proposals for mandatory repatriation, and it seems unlikely that they will go beyond French encouragement of repatriation through cash bonuses. In the fall of 1980, France and Algeria reached an agreement on Algerian emigrant worker repatriation that was hailed by French officials as a model return agreement. This recent Franco-Algerian agreement notwithstanding, it seems unlikely that large numbers of foreign workers will depart voluntarily in the near future. It will take some time to implement the return strategies now being discussed.

Since the recruitment halts, several other developments have complicated the foreign-worker issue. Illegal-alien populations estimated at 10

Table 2-5
Estimated Stocks of Foreign Workers, 1977

	Austria	Belgium	France	Germany	Luxembourg	Netherlands	Sweden	Switzerland
Algeria		3,600	331,100				200	
Austria				75,000			2,400	24,100
Finland				2,900			103,000	
Greece		8,900		162,500		1,900	9,200	4,800
Italy	2,100	119,000	199,200	281,200	10,800	10,000	2,800	253,100
Morocco		36,000	152,300	15,200		29,200	600	
Portugal		5,800	360,700	60,200	12,900	5,200	1,000	4,800
Spain		27,600	204,000	100,300	2,200	17,500	1,900	62,700
Tunisia		2,000	73,000			1,100	400	
Turkey	27,000	23,000	31,200	517,500		42,400	4,200	14,900
Yugoslavia	131,000		42,400	377,200	600	8,000	25,800	25,400
Others	28,800	143,900	109,600	296,600	22,600	21,000	73,800	103,000
Totals	188,900	369,800[a]	1,584,300[b]	1,888,600[c]	49,100	115,300	225,300	492,800[d]

Source: Système d' observation permanente des migrations, (Paris: Organization of Economic and Community Development, 1979).

[a]Frontier workers (daily commuters from neighborhing countries) not included.

[b]Based on 1975 20 percent census. May well represent an underestimation.

[c]Includes frontier workers.

[d]Does not include frontier or seasonal workers.

to 15 percent of total legal foreign populations apparently have grown significantly in recent years. The surge in illegal entrants has prompted European governments to require entry visas, even at the cost of straining bilateral relations, as in the German-Turkish case.[18] Turkey regards the reimposition of visa requirements upon its citizens by Germany as contravening its EEC associative status. France, Germany, and other countries have experienced large influxes of job seekers putatively posing as political refugees. Germany expected to receive more than 200,000 applications for political asylum in 1980 compared to 5,289 in 1973.[19] Abuse of Germany's liberal political asylum law was an important issue in the 1980 parliamentary election, and the German government has taken measures to prevent foreigners from circumventing the recruitment ban.[20] Critics of French refugee policy argue that it has become a virtual manpower policy enabling employers to hire Asian workers, perceived as more docile than nationals, at a time of high unemployment among resident French and foreign workers.[21]

The postwar evolution of Western European foreign-worker and immigration policies thus reveals important intra-European dissimilarities but broad policy convergence, especially in the cases of France, Switzerland, and the Federal Republic of Germany. The experiences of Great Britain, where immigrants automatically become citizens and receive voting rights, and Sweden, where almost half of the foreign work force is from neighboring and culturally similar Finland, are less germane to the question of an expanded U.S. temporary foreign-worker program. These three countries recruited most of postwar Europe's foreign workers and, with the limited exception of France, their foreign-labor policies are comparable to most proposed U.S. programs.

Notes

1. Georges Tapinos, *L'immigration étrangère en France* (Paris: Presses Universitaires de France, 1975), pp. 8-9.

2. Gary S. Cross, "The Structure of Labor Immigration into France between the Wars" (Ph.D. diss., University of Wisconsin, 1977), pp. 345-348.

3. H.J. Hoffman-Nowotny and Martin Killias, "Switzerland," in Ronald E. Krane, ed., *International Labor Migration in Europe* (New York: Praeger, 1979).

4. Albert Martens, *Les immigrés: Flux et reflux d'une main d'oeuvre d'appoint* (Louvain: Presses Universitaires de Louvain, n.d.).

5. Tapinos, *L'immigration étrangère*, pp. 33-34.

6. See table 4-1.

7. Société française pour le droit international, *Colloque de Clermont-Ferrand: Les travailleurs étrangers et le droit international* (Paris: Editions A. Pedone, 1979), pp. 169-170.

8. Ray C. Rist, "The European Economic Community (EEC) and Manpower Migrations: Policies and Prospects," *Journal of International Affairs* 33 (1979):201.

9. Tapinos, *L'immigration étrangère*, pp. 18-19.

10. Lionel Stoleru quoted in *Le nouveau journal*, October 6, 1978.

11. W.R. Böhning, "International Migration in Western Europe: Reflections on the Past Five Years," *International Labor Review* 118 (1979):401.

12. William Borders, "The Fire This Time for the British," *New York Times Sunday Magazine*, September 14, 1980, p. 50.

13. Frank Bovenkerk, "The Netherlands," in Krane, *International Labor Migration in Europe*, p. 131.

14. See Günter Graffenberger, "Auch Schweden hat Fremdarbeiter Probleme," *Tagesanzeiger* (Zurich), July 7, 1977, and "Confronting a Racial Time Bomb," *Time*, July 25, 1977.

15. See table 2-5. Also "Querelles d'amis sur le toit de l'Europe," *Le monde diplomatique* (December 1980).

16. Inter Nationes, *Social Report*, October 1976.

17. Luitz Dreesback, "Time Bomb Warning over Foreign Children," *German Tribune*, September 2, 1979, p. 4.

18. Marvine Howe, "Angry, Frustrated Turks Deplore West European Visa Restrictions," *New York Times*, November 5, 1980, and "West Germans' Visa Curbs Disturb Turkish Workers," *New York Times*, July 25, 1980, p. 3.

19. *Scala*, November 1980, p. 3.

20. Ellen Lentz, "Growing Influx of Third-World Refugees Stirs Debate in West Germany," *New York Times*, July 31, 1980.

3

Labor-Market Tests

Regulation of alien labor employment begins with decisions on the number of foreign workers permitted to enter and whether foreign-worker residency and type of employment will be restricted. Since regulation implies restriction of the number of aliens permitted entry for economic purposes, criteria must be established to determine legitimate need for foreign labor. Criteria also may be established to determine regional, industry-wide, or individual employer need. In France, Germany, and Switzerland, all employers must go through a certification procedure in order to be authorized to hire non-privileged (non-EEC) foreign labor. Until 1973, however, certification of need for employers seeking to hire foreigners for menial, physically difficult, or low-paid jobs was largely pro forma.

Most foreign-worker programs tie migrant workers to specific employers with one-year work contracts. All non-EEC workers are required to have a valid work contract before entering the labor-recruiting country, although France and Germany were known to permit foreigners who entered as tourists to obtain work and residence permits after they had arrived. Since the labor-recruiting government controls work contracts, it can regulate the number and location of its migrant workers.

Not all foreign nationals can be restricted with work permits. There are no numerical limits on the number of privileged foreign workers, who can enter a country freely and seek work. The free-movement provisions of the nine-nation EEC and the four-nation Nordic Common Labor Market guarantee most Western European nationals the right to live and work in neighboring countries on almost the same basis as citizens. Despite this free mobility, relatively few European nationals live and work in another European country.[1] In 1978, the two major groups of Common Market workers, the 104,000 Finns employed in Sweden and the 608,000 Italians employed in other EEC nations, comprised 14 percent of Western Europe's 5 million foreign workers. EEC and Nordic Common Labor Market nationals use friends, relatives, or state-run labor offices to find jobs in another member state. Public labor offices among member states cooperate by notifying each other of job vacancies—Germany, for example, informs Italy of its labor needs—although effective EEC cooperation in this area only recently seems to have gotten underway.[2]

Other categories of privileged foreign workers include a growing number of aliens who earned virtually unrestricted status through long periods of continuous residency in one country: ten years in France and Switzerland and eight years in Germany. France gradually has been stripping nationals from its former colonies of their privileged immigration status, although some nationals from former French colonies in Africa are still exempt from France's currently stringent restrictions on aliens.

How Many Migrants?

No nationwide ceilings have ever been placed on foreign-worker employment in France and Germany. Unfilled French and German job offers for low-skilled, physically difficult, or relatively low-paid occupations were routinely transmitted abroad. For Switzerland, job offers were routinely certified after foreign workers had already received contracts from Swiss employers. The only check on migrant recruitment was the rate of citizen (and later also resident foreign worker) unemployment. Changes in the annual influx of foreign workers to Germany are explained entirely by German unemployment rates until 1973. Much of the same was true of France, although many foreign workers in the 1960-1970 period found work outside the ambit of legal recruitment procedures and only subsequently were legalized.[3] When significant rates of unemployment were feared (in the case of Switzerland) or actually materialized (in France and Germany in the 1970s), recruitment of foreign workers (with a few exceptions) ceased.

France has a five-year indicative planning system in which manpower needs nationwide, by region, and by industry are estimated. Prior to 1973, French planners regularly projected physical and economic labor shortages, which, in turn, permitted calculation of optimal rates of foreign-labor recruitment. Although predicted labor shortages in the plans (along with broader demographic considerations) determined the nationwide need for foreign labor and justified the postwar policy of permitting employers to hire foreign workers, the actual inflow of foreign labor largely was unorganized or spontaneous and had little to do with the optimal rates of immigration suggested by the plans. Manpower projections in the plans served to open and sometimes close France's door to migrant labor, but the relationship between manpower plans and French migration policies was more theoretical than actual.

Some effort to quantify France's need for foreign labor was also apparent in the yearly quotas of legal migrants assigned to Portugal and Algeria. Between 1964 and 1968, Algeria was permitted to send 12,000 foreign laborers annually and after the 1968 Franco-Algerian accord 25,000 to 35,000 between 1968 and 1973. After the 1971 Franco-Portuguese labor accord, Portugal similarly was granted a quota of 65,000 annual openings, to the considerable displeasure of Algeria, which felt its privileged labor relationship with France depreciated. Again, however, the general inability of the French government to control labor migration prior to the general recruitment halt diminished the significance of quotas as quantitative expressions of need for foreign labor.[4]

Until the mid-1960s in Germany and Switzerland, there seems to have been no effort to determine the total need for foreign labor. Foreign-worker admissions were open-ended, a function of unfilled, primarily manual-labor job offers. Only after the emergence of a grass-roots protest movement did the Swiss government act to limit foreign-worker hiring. Initially the government urged voluntary restraint in hiring, but employers largely ignored the plea. In 1963, the Swiss government attempted to stop the hiring of additional foreign workers by freezing the foreign-worker shares of the work forces of individual firms, but this policy was frustrated when new foreign workers took jobs in industries being deserted by Swiss workers. Consequently the government decreed that firms had to reduce their employment of foreigners by 5 percent in both 1965 and 1966.[5]

Faced with the prospect of a referendum mandating reduction of the foreign population, Switzerland succeeded in stabilizing its foreign-worker population by setting ceilings on the total number of residency permits that would be authorized and by establishing yearly quotas on alien residency permits for each canton.[6] In 1975, cantonal allotments of work permits were cut significantly. Between 1964 and 1979, the number of seasonal work permit holders was reduced from its postwar high of 206,000 to 96,000. The Swiss Federal Council acting after a process of national consultation through the Federal Commission on the Foreigners' Question now determines acceptable ceilings of foreign labor. The ceilings are fixed with explicit references to sociopolitical factors, in addition to economic considerations.

Determination of nationwide need for foreign labor also can be influenced by labor-market conditions in labor-sending countries. Indeed, in some instances, such as the case of France and Algeria, determination of the yearly contingent of Algerian workers permitted to seek work in France was made with reference to labor-market conditions in both countries. However, as indicated by Western European decisions to halt foreign-labor recruitment without prior consultation of emigrant-sending countries, determination of labor needs took little account of labor-market conditions in Western Europe's partners to the south during the 1974-1975 recession.

Work and Residency Permit Systems

The elaborate Western European work and residency permit systems involve procedures to protect indigenous labor and certification of need by individual employers. Work permits provide authorization for aliens to take jobs (not all aliens are entitled to work), while residency permits authorize sojourns beyond the visiting period granted to aliens by virtue of their passports. (Appendix A summarizes certification procedures for non-privileged foreign workers in France, Germany, and Switzerland.)

As indicated by the growing number of privileged-status foreign workers not from the EEC, Western European countries have work and residency permit systems that progressively confer greater rights on migrants up to a legal status virtually commensurate with that of citizens except for the right to vote and hold public office. The defining attributes of privileged status are permanent or ordinarily nonrevocable residency rights and the elimination of any employment and geographical restrictions that may be imposed upon nonprivileged foreign workers. Western European work and residency permit systems have been considerably modified over the postwar period as the status of non-EEC foreign workers has been ameliorated.

France's work and residency permit systems were revised in 1975 and modified again in 1980. (References to France here and in appendixes A and K are to the system established in 1975. The most recent modifications are being implemented in 1981, so the specifics are not all discernible.) The thrust of the reform movement begun in 1975 was to simplify France's complex work and residency permit systems by synchronizing the length of work and residency permits, effectively combining these formerly uncoordinated authorizations, and by eliminating various special permits, notably those held by Algerians, so as to put all non-EEC, nonseasonal workers on the same administrative footing.

In all three countries, with the exceptions of privileged categories (including Algerians in France) and seasonal workers (whose permits are less than one year in duration), foreign workers initially received a one-year renewable work and residency authorization for employment with a specific employer. Residency rights were contingent on fulfillment of the labor contract. Germany and France have separate work and residency permits, and in Switzerland a residency permit contains employment authorization.

After completion of the initial one-year contract, foreign workers became free to switch employers. In Germany, the subsequent, usually synchronized, work and residency permits were valid for two or sometimes three years and could include occupational and geographical restrictions.[7] In France, the subsequent permit was valid for three years and usually included an employment restriction limiting the foreign worker to a specific occupation and a regional restriction on where employment could be sought. However, foreign workers were considerably less restricted geographically and vocationally after 1975 than before. In Switzerland, renewal of residency authorization was for one year only and, in most cases, was valid only for work in one canton and for a specific occupation.

After a period of continuous employment and residency, a foreign worker normally qualified for longer periods of work and residency authorization. In accord with a recommendation of the Organization of Economic Cooperation and Development (OECD), most foreign workers from OECD member states in the three countries were granted ordinarily nonrevocable work and residency rights after a five-year period of continuous work and residency. In other words, after five years, labor-market conditions could no longer be invoked to deny permit renewal. Despite general adherence to the recommendations of the OECD, to which all three countries belong, the mechanics of the respective work and residency permit systems vary considerably.

In Switzerland, a foreign worker usually would have to renew his or her one-year sojourn authorization four consecutive times before qualifying for preferential status and renewable two-year permits. After ten years of continuous residency, or less if married to a Swiss national, the worker would become eligible for an establishment authorization granting permanent residency rights that required renewal every three years. Establishment authorizations end all employment restrictions, except for a few jobs reserved for Swiss citizens, but are valid for one canton only. If an establishment authorization holder wished to move outside the canton, he or she could request establishment authorization from cantonal authorities.[8]

In Germany, most foreign workers received two-year work permits, called general permits, and corresponding two-year limited residence permits. To acquire the German residency permit, a foreign applicant had to have a work permit in hand. Sometimes problems arose; for example, applicants would not be hired without work permits, and work permits would not be issued without signed contracts. After renewal of the two-year general work permits and five years of continuous employment, migrants qualified for special work permits, issued regardless of labor-market conditions, that were valid for five years. Ordinarily there are no restrictions on the holders of special work permits, although some longer-term foreign workers may have encountered geographical restrictions due to a short-lived German policy (1975-1977) that permitted cities with large foreign-worker populations to bar further entry by foreign workers. After five years of continuous residence and the issuance of a special work permit, a foreign worker may obtain an unlimited residence permit if the worker can speak and understand rudimentary German, has suitable housing, and sends his or her children to German schools. A foreign worker becomes eligible for a residence title conferring permanent resident alien status after eight years of continuous residency. A worker must pass written and oral examinations in German and prove adaptation to German economic and social structures before being granted a residence title. Many foreign workers who qualify for the residence title do not apply for it because of plans to return home or unfamiliarity with administrative matters.[9]

Foreign workers in France now qualify for ten-year renewable work permits after four years of continuous work. Previously such permits were not granted, in many cases, until after fourteen years of continuous employment.[10] There are three French work permits. The so-called A or temporary work permit is given to migrants during their first year of employment, the B or ordinary work permit is given for renewable three-year periods, and the C work permit, valid for ten years, is renewable and has none of the employment and geographical restrictions that may be attached to permits A and B. As in Germany, a foreigner must have a valid work permit to qualify for a residency permit.

Before 1975, France had a parallel system of three residency permits, although they were not always synchronized with work permits. The temporary resident card was available to holders of A work permits, the ordinary resident card was available to holders of B work permits, and privileged residency cards were granted after ten years of continuous residency. Ten years of continuous residency with an ordinary resident permit also qualified a worker for a permanent work permit good for one occupation throughout France under the 1946 work permit system. Under the system instituted in 1975, longer-term workers were granted C permits valid for all salaried occupations anywhere in France but only for ten years, though with the possibility of renewal.

The work and residency permit systems are complicated further by special rules applying to the dependents of foreign workers. In Germany, where dependents can join foreign workers after one year, spouses can be granted work permits for employment in labor-short industries after four years of residency (after three years in acutely labor-deficient industries).[11] Children of foreign workers who came to Germany before age eighteen may be granted work permits after two years of residency. If foreign youths complete a vocational education course, the waiting period is waived. The children of five-year special permit holders are eligible to receive special work permits themselves up to age nineteen if the child has resided continuously in Germany for five years. In France, foreign-worker children who have been attending school in France for two to three years and have had a parent legally living in France for four years automatically qualify for ten-year C work permits. Spouses and other dependents with residency papers can apply for work through a special approval-for-employment procedure in which labor-market conditions are important criteria for rejection.[12] In Switzerland, where dependents ordinarily are entitled to join foreign workers after a twelve- to fifteen-month wait, legally resident spouses and children reaching work age may apply for work subject to labor-market conditions.

Protection of Indigenous Labor

The grant of employment authorization in all three countries is contingent upon satisfaction of various administrative criteria intended to safeguard the wages and working conditions of indigenous workers. Protective measures range from prohibiting foreign employment in certain kinds of jobs to giving indigenous workers priority over foreign workers if both apply for the same job. Employment officials have become much more stringent in protecting the employment priority of indigenous workers since 1973. Foreign workers with privileged or permanent status usually are considered indigenous workers.

A French law protecting the national work force was promulgated in 1932. Under its provisions, foreigners were barred from certain professions altogether, while quotas were established for foreigners in less-desirable sectors such as construction. In the postwar period, however, this 1932 law was not applied as foreign workers were funnelled into industries such as construction and automotive work where there were chronic labor shortages. Most foreign-worker admissions were routinely approved as long as proffered wages corresponded to collective wage agreements or administrators' notions of prevailing wages for the job category. All workers were covered by the minimum wage law. Since foreign workers were covered by labor laws, protection of working conditions was to be assured by labor law enforcement. Employers who abused foreign workers, thereby undercutting working conditions, could be refused authorization to hire foreigners in the future.

In Germany, foreign and domestic workers' wages were set by collective bargaining agreements. Proffered wages had to correspond to established wage scales. Migrants could not be admitted if working conditions would be undercut. Prior to the recruitment halt, most requests for foreign workers were routinely approved by local labor offices. While each request had to be examined on an individual basis, a de facto system of blanket certification for relatively low-paid, physically difficult, or menial jobs seems to have operated.

Like Germany but unlike France, Switzerland has a highly developed collective bargaining system that results in wage accords for entire industries. Foreign workers were routinely admitted for work in labor-short industries if the wages offered them corresponded to those set for a particular job in the collective agreements. Working conditions were stipulated in collective agreements.

During the economic expansion of the 1960s, there seems to have been little, if any, direct competition between foreign and native workers for

jobs. Hence, displacement was not an issue, and provisions giving indigenous workers priority over foreign workers seemed unnecessary. This
situation was dramatically altered in the 1970s. As shrinking employment
opportunities made displacement a potentially explosive issue, all three
countries instituted legal measures that granted indigenous workers, including privileged aliens, priority over foreign workers if both should apply
for the same job. Adverse labor-market conditions could be cited to deny
permit renewal to short-term migrants. While relatively few migrants seem
to have directly lost work and residency authorization because permits were
not renewed, the threat of nonrenewal weighed heavily on short-term
workers, and the resulting uncertainty contributed to decisions by many
such workers to return to their country of origin.

Employer, Industry, and Regional Certification

Employers had to convince government labor officials that native workers
were not available to fill job vacancies. Depending on the country,
employers could be required to advertise job offers and/or adapt production so that handicapped, aged, or part-time native workers could be
utilized.[13] Employers who hired illegal aliens could have their requests for
legal foreign workers denied. Employers also had to attest that a foreign
employee would be adequately housed. Violation of housing, wage, or
working condition agreements all constituted grounds for denying any
future employer requests for foreign labor.

Except for certain jobs expressly reserved to citizens, largely in the
public domain, foreign workers could be employed in virtually any industry. In reality, foreign workers were admitted in large numbers only into
industries with relatively low-paid and low-skilled, boring, or physically ar-
duous jobs. The construction industry, assembly-line manufacturing, and
textiles benefited from de facto blanket certifications for alien employment
in bottom-rung work. Work permits could keep foreigners in labor-short industries for periods of up to five years, and sometimes longer in France. In
the 1970s, foreign-worker employment remained concentrated in certain industries, but more and more foreign workers qualified for unrestricted permits and moved into other sectors of the economy.

Permit systems also gave Western European governments hypothetical
control over the location of many foreign workers. The Swiss have the most
developed system to make regional allocation of foreign labor. Each canton
has a foreign-worker quota. In 1979, the canton of Geneva, for example,
received 2,000 additional authorizations because of its rapid economic
growth.[14] However, despite the legal ability to restrict foreign-worker job
and geographic mobility, foreign-worker populations are spatially concentrated in all three countries.

In Germany, 50 percent of the foreign population lives on less than 4 percent of the territory. In France, 34 percent of all foreigners live in the Paris region. The canton of Zurich alone holds one-fifth of the foreign population of Switzerland.[15] Foreign-worker spatial concentrations are largely explained by the concentrated nature of the jobs available to these workers. German authorities moved to halt the process of urban concentration (or, according to some, "ghettoization") by allowing major cities to forbid the further in-migration of foreign workers once the foreign component of the total population passed 12 percent. This controversial administrative measure was dropped, although it apparently still is in effect in some West Berlin neighborhoods, in 1977 after ILO officials suggested that it was contrary to ILO conventions concerning migrant labor that Germany had ratified. In France, the notion of a tolerance level (*seuil de tolerance*) is used unofficially to limit further migrant concentration in some urban areas, especially in the Paris region. If the tolerance level is deemed surpassed, (unwritten) administrative orders may bar foreigners from public housing in order to restrain the growth of the foreign population.

Assessment

Low unemployment rates through much of the postwar period coupled with the assumption that most foreign workers would return home during economic downturns precluded the development of elaborate labor-market testing techniques. The number of job vacancies and the unemployment rate determined aggregate need. When recruitment was halted, there were still job vacancies but also growing unemployment. Sociopolitical factors, whose potential was largely ignored in decisions to admit foreign workers prior to 1970, weighed heavily in decisions to stop recruitment by 1973-1974.

In a depressed economic situation with relatively high unemployment (1981 French and German unemployment rates were 6.9 and 4.5 percent, respectively, compared to 8 percent in the United States), there is no serious possibility that recruitment will be resumed despite continuing labor shortages in some relatively low-paid, menial jobs and calls by some employers for a resumption of recruitment.[16] New foreign workers—the dependents of established migrants—have taken jobs, and some limited exceptions to recruitment bans have been made. Unrest over unemployment, particularly youth joblessness, along with significant foreign-worker integration problems, however, make a resumption of recruitment politically unfeasible even if it might have some limited economic justification or some long-term demographic rationale.

Assessment of how well Western European governments have protected the interests of indigenous labor while responding to employers' personnel shortages and overall economic needs is partly a function of time. Prior to 1973, foreign-worker recruitment seemed to serve everyone's interests. Indeed many native workers found employment in better-paying, more socially prestigious jobs because of the general economic boom enhanced by foreign workers. In the 1960s, it was widely assumed that foreign workers took jobs that native workers no longer wanted and jobs that could not be filled because of general labor shortages. But growing unemployment in the mid-1970s and the realization that millions of foreign workers and their dependents had become permanent residents who would not voluntarily depart made the almost uniformly positive assessments of the 1960s appear shortsighted. Displacement of citizens by foreign labor became an issue. Unemployment rates were blamed, in part, on the presence of foreign workers. Similarly, the overall economic benefits of foreign labor employment began to be questioned as social expenditures for foreign populations increased.

Defenders of foreign workers pointed out that migrants had become a structural or permanent part of the work force and that plans to force or entice foreign workers to go home would have untoward economic effects since indigenous workers could not be substituted for most foreign workers. While statements in favor of massive substitution were illusory because of legal and diplomatic circumstances, the small-scale French effort to substitute indigenous workers for foreign workers in manual-labor jobs met with only limited success. This program, called *révalorisation du travail manuel*, gave incentives to firms which hired French workers for manual labor and generally sought to improve wages and working conditions for manual-labor workers. The program was specifically designed to counteract problems stemming from massive recruitment of alien workers in the 1960s.

In part, efforts to attract indigenous workers to manual-labor jobs were impeded by the relatively poor working conditions and social stigma attached to jobs where foreign labor was concentrated. Despite stipulations that foreign-worker admissions not undercut working conditions, many job categories in which foreigners concentrated experienced relative declines in working conditions and, to a lesser extent, in wages.[17] Adverse effects of massive foreign-worker employment upon industry were most apparent in the French construction industry where wage levels and working conditions steadily deteriorated to the point that by the late 1970s the inability of employers to hire skilled workers threatened the economic viability of many firms.[18] The most important factor of job depreciation seemed to be the social stigma attached to jobs identified with foreign workers. It remains to be seen whether unemployment pressures will overcome social barriers to Western Europeans' accepting the kinds of jobs held by many foreign workers.

Foreign-worker admissions were conditional upon wage and housing standards designed to uphold socioeconomic norms, to ensure foreign workers equality, and to prevent foreign workers from depressing the wages and working conditions of citizens. How well Western European governments enforced these standards is a matter of considerable controversy. Lax housing enforcement and labor-law violations in nonunionized industries with concentrations of foreign workers in France have been considerable problems. In all three countries, some foreign workers complained of receiving lower wages for work equal to that of higher-paid citizen workers. Social depreciation of jobs in some labor categories in which foreign workers were concentrated suggests that socioeconomic norms were undercut. Still, in many other cases, particularly in heavily unionized industries, enforcement of admission criteria was vigorous. Generally it can be said that as integration problems became more salient and unions, churches, and political parties paid more attention to foreign labor, enforcement of admission standards improved.

Notes

1. Heinz Werner, "Migration and Free Movement of Workers in Western Europe" in Philipe Bernard, ed., *Les travailleurs étrangers en Europe occidentale* (Paris: Mouton, 1976).

2. Interview with G. Callovi, directorate-general for employment and social affairs, EEC, Spring 1980.

3. G. Tapinos, *L'immigration étrangère en France* (Paris: Presses Universitaires de France, 1975), p. 65.

4. Interview with Cessieux, Manpower Section, Eighth Plan, Commissariat du Plan, Summer 1980.

5. Werner, "Migration and Free Movement of Workers," p. 73.

6. Congressional Research Service, *Temporary Worker Programs: Background and Issues* (Washington, D.C.: U.S. Government Printing Office, 1980), pp. 88-89.

7. Elmar Hönekopp and Hans Ullman, *The Effect of Immigration on Social Structures* (Nuremberg: Institute for Labor Market Research Paper, 1980), pp. 13, 19.

8. Fédération suisse des bourgeoises, Association des communes suisses and union des villes suisses, *Les étrangers dans la commune* (Bern: Commission fédérale pour les problèmes des étrangers, 1979), p. 14.

9. E. Hönekopp and H. Ullman, *The Effect of Immigration on Social Structures* (Nuremberg: Institute for Labor Market Research, 1980), pp. 11-23.

10. Direction de la Population et des migrations, *Le dossier de l'immigration*, 5th ed. (Paris: Ministère du travail et de la participation, November 1978), Entry 4.

11. Hönekopp and Ullman, *Effect of Immigration*, pp. 29-31.

12. Directorate-General, Employment and Social Affairs, *Comparative Survey of Conditions and Procedures for Admission of Third Country Workers for Employment in the Member States* (Brussels: Commission of the European Communities, 1980), p. 8.

13. See, for example, Hönekopp and Ullman, *Effect of Immigration*, p. 18.

14. *Journal de Genève*, September 13, 1979.

15. Interagency Task Force on Immigration Policy, *Staff Report* (Washington, D.C.: Departments of Justice, State, and Labor, 1979), p. 517.

16. Georg Heller, "Industry Urges End to Ban on Hiring of Migrant Workers," *German Tribune*, September 16, 1975, p. 5.

17. See Robert Weisz, Michel Anselme, Norbert Sultan, and Hocine Tandjaoui, "Repartition des postes et segmentation du marché du travail: le cas du BTP," mimeographed (Aix-en-Provence: Institut d'administration des entreprises, 1978), pp. 150-151.

18. See, Raphäel-Emmanuel Verhaeren, *Immigration et Force de Travail dans le B.T.P.* (Grenoble: Institut de Recherche Economique et de Planification, 1976).

4 The Diplomatic Underpinnings of Western European Foreign-Worker Policies

Consistent with the legal doctrine of national sovereignty, Western European states reserve final authority in all matters concerning the admission, residence, and departure of foreign nationals, including migrant workers, on their soil. Elementary human rights possessed by all persons aside, any rights and privileges possessed by foreign workers are granted by the European host states. A universal right of free labor mobility is not recognized. Free movement of labor occurs only in the context of the EEC and the Nordic Common Labor Market as the result of multilateral treaties extending reciprocal rights and privileges to the nationals of the treaty signatories. Illegal aliens in Western Europe do not enjoy the rights and privileges possessed by legal foreign workers. However, illegal aliens have the basic human rights of all persons that are recognized, if not always protected.

Western European governments generally authorize foreign-worker employment rather than legalize it post facto or tolerate illegal-alien employment. Since foreign nationals are involved, authorization has taken place through bilateral and multilateral diplomatic devices that range from the provisions guaranteeing free labor mobility in far-ranging treaties such as the Treaty of Rome, which established the EEC in 1957, to bilateral accords pertaining only to the recruitment of foreigners for employment in a Western European country. The international character of migrant labor and the anomalous condition of working and living in a country without being a constituent member or citizen of it has made the employment, legal status, and sociopolitical dimensions of migrant labor an important focus of study for international and regional organizations. By virtue of membership in or adherence to the instruments of international and regional organizations, Western European governments have been influenced by international and regional organization recommendations on foreign labor. Consequently, consideration of the diplomatic underpinnings of Western European foreign-worker policies must pay close attention to the evolution of international and regional organizational stances on migrant workers, in addition to multilateral treaties and bilateral labor accords.

The Historical Context

Europe's postwar migrant labor flows were not unprecedented. Many foreign workers in Western Europe during the interwar period were recruited under the aegis of bilateral labor agreements. The ILO, founded in 1919 as part of the Versailles Treaty as a specialized adjunct to the League of Nations, was expressly charged with facilitating international labor transfers and monitoring migrant-worker socioeconomic conditions. During the interwar period, the ILO, in conjunction with the League of Nations, took an active role in gathering information on bilateral labor programs and in proposing conventions and recommendations applicable to migrant workers. While the ILO and the League of Nations met with only limited success in securing equal treatment for migrant workers, both organizations influenced the trend that made treaties or formal diplomatic agreements the basis of international labor migration. Since the interwar period, a treaty or some other formal diplomatic agreement has been the accepted international norm for authorization of foreign-worker employment.

The special role of the ILO in migrant worker matters was reaffirmed at the Philadelphia Conference in 1944, which revitalized the ILO and made it an autonomous adjunct to the nascent United Nations. In 1949, the tripartite plenary session or conference of the ILO approved convention 97 and recommendation 86 concerning migration for employment. (See appendix B.) These instruments constituted the fundamental sources of postwar international norms concerning regulation of international labor migration and strongly influenced postwar Western European foreign-labor policies. The convention included standards pertaining to the recruitment of migrants, specified the responsibilities of governments and private employers, and, more generally, held forth the principle of equality of treatment between citizens and foreign workers as the only legitimate basis for governmental policies toward migrant workers. Three annexes were attached to convention 97 to deal with recruitment not organized by governments, governmentally organized recruitment, and arrangements for personal possessions of the migrant workers. In both annexes I and II, governments are charged with strict regulation of migrant-worker recruitment and employment in order to protect migrants.

Recommendation 86 called on governments to facilitate the international distribution of manpower from labor-surplus to labor-deficit countries. An annex contains a model bilateral agreement for temporary or permanent labor migration. Under sections IV and V of recommendation 86, family members of foreign workers admitted for nontemporary work were to be allowed entry and employment rights and, as far as possible, restrictions on foreign workers and their dependents were to cease after five years of residency abroad.

ILO conventions, in effect international treaties if ratified by a member state, are binding, and compliance is monitored through a procedure of reporting and consultation. Member states can make representations (or allege noncompliance) by another ILO member state if duties are not fulfilled. ILO recommendations are less powerful than conventions since they are not binding but rather contain guidelines to which member countries are invited to refer in shaping national policies. Implementation of recommendations, however, is encouraged by many of the same supervisory procedures used in the case of conventions. Recommendations are submitted to appropriate authorities in all member states for their consideration, and reports may be required of members to ascertain what measures have been taken to implement a recommendation. ILO labor standards (a generic term for conventions and recommendations) apply to all employees within a member state unless particular reference is made—for example, to noncitizen employees.[1]

Convention 97 (see appendix C) was ratified in its entirety by the Federal Republic of Germany in 1959 and, with the exception of annex II, by France in 1954. Switzerland has not ratified the convention, but its postwar foreign-worker policies were indirectly influenced by the Geneva-based ILO. Hence, convention 97 and recommendation 86 played a major role in shaping postwar Western European foreign-worker policies. Convention 97 provided for migrant orientation and assistance prior to and after departure, action against misleading publicity, such as placing erroneous job offers in newspapers, appropriate medical services, and authorization for a migrant to transfer earnings home. Article 6 of the convention obliges labor-recruiting countries to treat migrants equally in the areas of employment rights, including trade union membership, social security, employment taxes, and legal proceedings.

Convention 97 and recommendation 86 were supplemented in 1955 by ILO recommendation 100 concerning the protection of migrant workers in less-developed countries and in 1962 by convention 118 pertaining to equal treatment in social security. Although the ILO constantly monitored foreign-worker affairs in Western Europe and provided technical assistance to regional organizations and individual governments on migrant matters, its next major interventions on migrant worker matters did not occur until the 1970s. During the hiatus between 1949 and 1975, when the ILO approved convention 143 and recommendation 151 concerning migrants in abusive conditions and equality of migrant opportunity and treatment, significant diplomatic developments affecting foreign workers in Western Europe had taken place on the level of regional organizations and multilateral treaties.

The OECD

The Organization for Economic Cooperation and Development (OECD) grew out of the seventeen-nation Organization for European Economic

Cooperation (OEEC), established in 1948 to coordinate implementation of the Marshall Plan. The OECD, which came into being in 1960 and is based in Paris, currently has twenty-four members, including the United States, France, the Federal Republic of Germany, and Switzerland, along with such major labor-sending countries as Turkey, Italy, Greece, Spain, and Portugal. The aims of the OECD have been summarized as follows: "To promote economic and social welfare throughout the OECD area by coordinating member country policies to that end, to contribute to the good functioning of the world economy notably by stimulating and harmonizing its members' efforts in favor of developing countries."[2] The OECD's primary diplomatic instruments are decisions, which are binding upon member countries, and recommendations, which suggest guidelines but are not binding. OECD members, however, may be required to make reports on the measures they have undertaken to implement a recommendation.

OEEC-OECD involvement in migrant-worker matters stems from article 8 of the convention on European Economic Cooperation of April 18, 1948. This article calls upon signatories to facilitate the movement of workers between them so as to rationalize manpower usage. The signatories promised to cooperate in reducing barriers to free movement of labor in a progressive, gradual manner. On the basis of article 8, the Manpower Committee of the OEEC, later to become the Committee on Manpower and Social Affairs of the OECD, was established to pursue the goal of manpower cooperation. In 1953, the OECD adopted a decision pertaining to the employment of nationals from member states, which effectively implemented article 8. Although subsequently amended, this 1953 decision included key provisions that shaped the course of Western European foreign-worker policies, particularly in the case of non-EEC Switzerland. Most notably, the 1953 OECD decision as amended included a provision that nationals from member countries should be allowed to fill one-month-old vacancies in any OECD member state and that, after five years of continuous residency, restrictions on foreign workers from another OECD state normally should end.[3]

In 1961, the OECD turned its attention to foreign workers from nonmember states and adopted a recommendation concerning their introduction and employment that followed the contours of the ILO's convention 97 and recommendation 86. The next major OECD instrument concerning foreign workers was not adopted until 1976. This recommendation, on global employment and manpower policy, adopted March 5, 1976, reflected the notion of migratory chains developed by the OECD: the need to promote migrant training to enable migrants to return home and contribute to the economic development of their native societies. This new emphasis on return and migrant training was due, in part, to the realization that foreign-worker policies in the 1960s and early 1970s had largely ignored the development needs of emigrant-sending nations.[4]

The Council of Europe

Created by the statute signed in London in 1949 by ten noncommunist European states, including France, the Council of Europe's aim is "to achieve a greater unity between its members for the purpose of safeguarding and realizing the ideals and principles which are their common heritage and facilitating their economic and social progress."[5] The council, which is headquartered in Strasbourg, has since grown to twenty members, including the Federal Republic of Germany as of 1950 and Switzerland as of 1963. Among major emigrant-sending countries, Italy was a founding member of the council, while Greece and Turkey became members in 1949 and 1950, respectively. Spain and Portugal have joined recently.

The Council of Europe has two major organs: the Committee of Ministers, the executive, intergovernmental body made up of one designated minister from each member state, and the Consultative Assembly, the deliberative body comprised of delegates chosen or appointed on an approximate proportional basis wherein more-populous members have larger national delegations but all members have at least three delegates. The primary diplomatic instruments of the Council of Europe are conventions, agreements, and protocols, which are approved by the Council of Ministers for signature by member states and, consequently, are binding if ratified. Recommendations are unanimous resolutions of the Council of Ministers and therefore are authoritative but not formally binding statements of joint policy. Member states may be required to report their progress on the implementation of any Council of Ministers instrument. The Consultative Assembly may pass recommendations, which must be acted upon by the Council of Ministers, or it may adopt resolutions, which do not require executive organ action but which express the majority opinion of this deliberative body.

The importance attached to the migrant-worker issue within the Council of Europe is long-standing. The Convention for the Protection of Human Rights and Fundamental Freedoms, signed in 1950 with a protocol added in 1952, ensured the basic rights of all persons under the jurisdication of ratifying states, although this convention did not provide for an unconditional or universal right of entry. In 1955, the European Convention of Establishment was opened up to ratification. This convention included provisions that gave all foreigners, not only migrant workers, judicial status and that facilitated entry and free circulation for nationals from member states as long as their stay was temporary and did not harm national interests.

In 1961, the European Social Charter was signed. Two articles of this convention were of particular importance: article 18, which was not a common denominator clause (that is, it could be excluded by a ratifying state) and article 19. Article 18 essentially reiterated the sense of the European

Establishment Convention in that signatories promised to facilitate entry from member states, simplify and abolish procedures and special taxes for foreign workers, and similar provisions. Article 19, however, was more far-ranging in that it contained a number of measures designed to govern the arrival and departure of migrant workers and their families. Council of Europe conventions concerned only foreign workers from member states.[6]

The most important Council of Europe project on behalf of migrant workers is the European Convention on the Legal Status of Migrant Workers, which was submitted to the Council of Ministers in 1971 and, after protracted negotiations, finally was signed in 1977. The convention is aimed at guaranteeing foreign workers from member states, to the fullest measure possible, equal treatment with national work forces in matters concerning working and living conditions. Specific provisions of the convention pertain to housing, vocational training, the education of migrant children, working conditions, social security, work accidents, union rights, residency rights, and family-reunion rights among others. After considerable controversy, seasonal workers were excluded from this convention.[7]

Appendix D presents the French, Swiss, and German ratification records on major Council of Europe conventions concerning migrant workers. In several instances, conventions have been almost implemented, but relatively minor disagreements and technicalities are holding up formal ratification. Even if they are not implemented, however, all Council of Europe instruments influence foreign-worker policy because they influence public opinion. In addition to the conventions signed thus far, the Council of Ministers has adopted resolutions concerning better migrant language training, vocational training, equality of treatment, model contracts, and schooling for migrant children.[8] One consequence of resolutions has been to diminish policy variations among the three countries under consideration in this book. Of late, the Council of Europe, in liason with the Council of European Communities, has been considering the political status of foreign workers, especially the feasibility of their voting in local elections.

The EEC

The influence of the ILO, the OECD, and, to a lesser extent, the Council of Europe upon the six founding states of the European Economic Community in the realm of migrant-labor-policy matters was considerable; however, the Treaty of Rome is the most important diplomatic document authorizing postwar labor migrations to France and Germany. Articles 48 and 49 provided, respectively, for free movement of labor between EEC members and an end to discrimination against noncitizen EEC workers. These provisions were to be progressively implemented over a ten-year period after 1957.

The original six-member EEC expanded to nine members in 1972 (see appendix E). Greece became the tenth EEC member in 1981. Turkey, Spain, and Portugal all have EEC associate status which confers preferential treatment in economic matters, and the last two states currently are being considered for full membership. While the focus of EEC cooperation is on the economic integration of member states, significant cooperation on domestic and foreign political and social matters also has evolved. Indeed the founding of the EEC was prompted as much by the long-term political goal of European unity as it was by economic considerations. Economic integration was to pave the way for political integration. Free movement of labor responded to postwar economic exigencies, including chronic labor shortages in Germany, France, and the Benelux countries, coupled with chronic unemployment in Italy, and to political aspirations (EEC workers would cement diplomatic engagements and be the precursors of European citizens).

In view of the political and economic goals of the EEC, it is understandable that EEC foreign workers would be granted privileged status vis-à-vis foreign workers from non-EEC countries. Even in 1959, though, only 48 percent of all foreign workers in the EEC were from other EEC members.[9] Since then, the proportion of EEC to third-country foreign workers has dropped steadily. In 1978, only 27 percent of all foreign workers were from member states. Of these, Italian and Irish emigrant workers (totaling 800,000 and 450,000, respectively, in 1974) constituted the bulk of community workers.[10] Overall, the provision for free movement of labor has resulted in relatively modest labor migration between EEC members.

Implementation of articles 48 and 49 occurred in three stages.[11] In 1961, regulation 15/61 was adopted granting workers from EEC countries the right to take a job in another member country if the job remained vacant three weeks after being posted by a labor office and if national workers were unavailable. EEC regulations are immediately binding upon member states and are promulgated by the Council of Ministers, the EEC's executive organ, or, in most cases, by the Commission, the EEC's secretariat, which also is invested with executive power. Other EEC instruments include *directives,* which are legally binding but which give member states several years to harmonize national legislation, *decisions,* which are similar to directives but usually relate to individual cases, and *recommendations* or *opinions,* which are not legally binding but do exert moral pressure.

Regulation 15/61, hence, superseded contrary national legislation. Under its provisions, EEC workers were to receive one-year renewable work permits for a specified industry or occupation. After three years of employment, job restrictions were ended, and after four years, unrestricted permits were issued and the worker's status was to be assimilated to that of a native worker. Regulation 15/61 also established the European Office for Coordination, which was to become a community-wide labor exchange but which became more of a monitoring agency for compliance with regulation 15/61. According to EEC sources, a community-wide labor exchange is only now becoming effective. Regulation 15/61 did not apply to workers from colonies and overseas territories.

Encouraged by the successful implementation of regulation 15/61, the EEC promulgated regulation 38/64 in 1964, which eliminated the three-week waiting period and allowed member states to restrict EEC members from taking jobs only in designated labor-surplus occupations. Guidelines concerning legal and social rights of community workers were stipulated that effectively gave these workers equal rights once hired. It was also specified that community workers should be allowed to have their families accompany them. Member states were to be given fifteen-day notice of a labor vacancy before a non-EEC worker could be recruited.

Adoption of regulation 1612/68 in 1968 fully implemented articles 48 and 49 of the Treaty of Rome and, as buttressed by regulations 360/68 and 1251/70, constitutes the present legal basis for community worker employ-ment. Under regulation 1612, community workers are no longer restricted to jobs posted in labor offices, and housing requirements attached to their employment, such as measures obliging employers to secure adequate housing for alien workers prior to receiving authorization to employ the aliens, were abolished. Hence, unlike non-EEC workers (with the major exceptions in the French case of Algerians until 1973 and some privileged nationality groups from ex-colonies in sub-Sahara Africa), EEC nationals are not required to obtain work and residency permission prior to emigrating for economic purposes.

EEC nationals have three months in which to look for work, and after finding a job, are automatically entitled to five-year renewable employment and residency authorization. There are no restrictions placed on EEC foreign workers except that they may be barred from employment in the public sector and in certain designated labor-surplus jobs, and they cannot vote or hold public office in the political institutions of the host society. EEC workers also are subject to deportation in criminal cases and under ill-defined and infrequently used powers reserved to member states in the area of national security. Community workers may be permitted to vote in elections for the European parliament, but France and Germany do not allow EEC workers to vote for French or German delegates to the parliament. Instead they encourage EEC workers to participate in their own respective national elections and, to this end, approved consular voting for resident EEC workers.

In 1974, the EEC began consideration of a proposed Action Program in Favor of Migrant Workers and Their Families, which was formally adopted as a resolution in 1976. This document contained guidelines applicable to non-EEC workers and their dependents throughout EEC. The primary aim of the program was to promote the integration of non-EEC workers by ameliorating their socioeconomic status through the "progressive elimination of discriminations," thereby narrowing the gap between community workers and non-EEC foreign workers.[12] Specific provisions of the resolution ranged from the creation or expansion of information programs aimed at fostering better foreign-worker-citizen relations to improving migrant vocational training and education of migrant children. While the Action Program resolution left considerable leeway for dissimilar interpretation by member states, it has had the effect of standardizing national policies toward migrant workers throughout the EEC and between non-EEC and EEC nationals. (Non-EEC worker recruitment has been halted since 1973-1974; EEC nationals and seasonal workers are not subject to the bans.)

The importance of the migrant-labor issue to the EEC has been underscored in recent negotiations concerning EEC expansion. Greek workers will not enjoy unrestricted mobility rights until 1988. Negotiations between strategically important Turkey and the EEC have shown little progress to date largely because Germany fears a massive emigration of Turks. Recent French and German reimposition of visa requirements upon Turkish citizens has stirred considerable resentment in Turkey and has prompted charges that the new visa requirements contravene Turkey's associative status with the EEC. Spain and Portugal each have a half-million nationals employed in EEC countries, posing potential migration problems if they are to join the EEC. However, negotiations with Spain have been hampered mainly by French fears of agricultural competition, not by fears of a massive inflow of foreign workers, as in the case of Turkey.

The influence of EEC membership upon the formulation of French and German foreign-worker policies is not limited to the adoption of documents. Because of the broad intersocietal links fostered in large part by the EEC (and also by the Council of Europe), both the French and German governments are sensitive to developments in migrant-worker matters across the Rhine. The policies of either country never are greatly out of step with those of the other, although French officials frequently suggest that German policies are less liberal or humane. These largely erroneous assertions concerning Germany attempt to undercut domestic criticism of French policies toward foreign labor. In reality, Germany is as liberal as France in foreign-worker matters, and perhaps more so. The only major exception is in the area of naturalization procedures, where France clearly has been less restrictive.

The Franco-African Community

In addition to community workers and long-term migrants who have earned privileged status, Algerian and black African workers in France constitute the most sizable groups of foreign workers who benefited from special status as a result of broader diplomatic engagements. Due to the particular importance of the Franco-Algerian case, it is useful to treat the two privileged groups from ex-French possessions separately, although both groups were admitted through special procedures and were not required to sign a contract and obtain work authorization before going to France. Algerians and nationals from the Franco-African community also are not required to have separate work and residency permits. Instead, their residency permits, if they have found work, are stamped "salaried worker."

Unlike the case of Algeria, whose workers emigrated to the French mainland in large numbers prior to independence, French colonies in sub-Saharan Africa did not have significant emigrant worker communities on mainland France when they acceded to independence.[13] Like many Algerians, however, tens of thousands of black Africans had served in the French army. In part because of these past military contributions but also because of General de Gaulle's vision of close Franco-African cooperation in the postindependence era, title XII of the constitution of the Fifth Republic created the Franco-African Community. As one former colony after the other acceded to independence, several either signed a multilateral treaty with France or a similar bilateral treaty. (See colums 1 and 2 of appendix F.) Whether multilateral or bilateral, these treaties were signed in the optic of the Franco-African Community and allowed nationals of the signatories freedom of movement to and establishment in France. All of these treaties included a clause assimilating ex-colonials to French citizens with regard to employment rights. In 1963, the French government extended the same rights to nationals from all former black African colonies (with the exception of Sekou Touré's Guinea) regardless of whether they had signed the 1960-style treaties.[14] Hence, just about all black Africans from ex-French colonies enjoyed privileged status during the 1960s.

Initially to the surprise of French officials and eventually to their consternation, tens of thousands of Black Africans, mainly from the predominantly Muslim Soninké ethnic group, which lives along the Senegal River in Mauritania, Mali, and Senegal, emigrated during the 1960s. By the early 1970s, there were an estimated 70,000 black African workers in France.[15] These almost exclusively male emigrants concentrated in certain neighborhoods in major urban centers and in characteristic jobs—street sweeping, automobile manufacture, and handicraft peddling. The Soninké and several other ethnic groups that emigrated in large numbers live communally and do so in France as well. Consequently they often live in overcrowded, rundown housing. To French officials, the health and integration problems due to the inadaptation of black African workers to French society necessitated revision of the privileged status of black ex-colonials in migration matters. Revision also was given momentum as the Gaullist ideal of Franco-African community faded and was replaced by a more pragmatic conception of Franco-African ties.

In the early 1970s, the Ministry of Foreign Affairs undertook a broad effort to renegotiate bilateral accords so as to discontinue the privileged status of black ex-colonials and to place them on an equal footing with nationals from other recruitment countries. This diplomatic effort is still underway. (Former colonies that signed treaties requiring emigrants to receive work authorization prior to departure are listed in column 4 of appendix F.) Black Africans continued to be free to visit France as they wished, however, and French officials found it difficult to prevent their illegal employment. In 1974, a more restrictive type of circulation treaty was proposed by the French government and eventually approved by the African governments listed in column 5 of appendix F. However, many of these 1974-type treaties have not become fully effective. The 1974-type treaties required the concerned black African nationality groups to have valid passports and valid residency permits. The treaties also placed controls on students and family members from the countries concerned. As of 1978, nationals from Benin, the Camerouns, Congo (Brazzaville), the Ivory Coast, Mali, Niger, Senegal, and Togo, which all signed the 1974-type treaty, still were not required to have visas to visit France and, if employed, they did not need a separate work permit but rather had to have residency permits approved for work by having them stamped "salaried worker."[16]

The French found the effort to downgrade the privileged status of emigrant workers from ex-colonies in black Africa diplomatically difficult. Nonetheless, the French government remains confident that it will succeed in downgrading black African workers to a status equal to that of non-privileged foreign workers from countries like Morocco. Negotiations with former black African colonies to this end have been very sensitive and are sometimes impaired by external events, such as the recent brutal murder of several Senegalese in Orange. The French experience underscores the point that special relationships in migrant-worker matters are more difficult to change or to terminate than to start.

Bilateral Accords

Most of the foreign workers in the three countries under consideration were not admitted as privileged-status foreign workers under the terms of far-ranging multilateral treaties. Rather, their entry was authorized under bilateral agreements specifically negotiated to regulate labor migration. While bilateral labor accords are narrowly focused in that they pertain only to labor migration, they are not without broader diplomatic significance; inevitably they affect overall diplomatic relations in cases where significant numbers of workers are employed abroad. When Western European bilateral manpower agreements were first signed, it was assumed that they would be beneficial to the emigrant-sending and -receiving countries alike. With time, the soundness of this assumption concerning the mutually beneficial effects of labor migration increasingly has been questioned, and, in several instances, migrant-labor programs have been a source of strain in bilateral relations, most notably in the Franco-Algerian, Germano-Turkish and Italy-Swiss cases.

Western European bilateral labor agreements with emigrant labor-sending nations generally conformed to the international norms established by the ILO's convention 97 and recommendation 86, the OEEC/OCDE's 1953 decision concerning the employment of nationals from member states, and the various conventions proposed by the Council of Europe. Consequently, most treaties contain similar requirements for translated contracts, signature of contracts prior to departure, and specification of the host society's role in recruitment, transportation costs, medical examinations, family entry, adequate housing, and equality of treatment. The focus of bilateral labor accords was upon recruitment procedures. Except for equality-of-treatment clauses, the status of migrants once they had taken up employment was largely excluded from bilateral negotiations.

In part, this avoidance of postrecruitment issues stemmed from a shared desire not to infringe upon the politically delicate prerogatives of sovereign states. Additionally, however, bilateral commissions were established to monitor implementation of the accords and to work out problems that arose.[17] Hence, provision was made for bilateral cooperation in the postrecruitment stage, but very little was formally agreed upon except that foreign workers should receive equality of treatment, a vague provision that did not commit host governments to specific actions in favor of migrant workers.

If bilateral labor agreements tended to resemble one another in their focus on recruitment procedures and vagueness on postrecruitment issues, there were significant variations among the texts. Most bilateral treaties, for example, left the question of the total number of workers to be recruited open, to be determined by host-society authorities in view of their employment situation. Some bilateral accords, however, set yearly quotas of workers to be admitted. This was the case of France-Algeria and Germany-Tunisia. Only the Franco-Algerian accord of 1964 stipulates that the quantity of foreign workers to be admitted should be determined in relation to the employment situations of both the sending and receiving countries.[18]

The texts of treaties also vary considerably with regard to family entry. The Franco-Spanish treaty, for example, mentions that "the French government looks with favor upon the admission of the spouse and children . . . of permanent Spanish workers in France." In the Franco-

Moroccan and Franco-Tunisian treaties, the text is significantly different: "the French government accords all facilities within the limits of the law and regulations in effect, to the families of Tunisian [Moroccan] workers which wish to join the latter in France."[19] Consequently, in the Tunisian and Moroccan cases, the French engagement to permit family entry could be interpreted as being contingent upon laws or regulations that conceivably could block family entry. In the Franco-Portuguese case, despite a clear-cut French treaty commitment to permit family entry, the French government in 1977 attempted to block further family entry by issuing a regulation. The ban on Portuguese family entry, however, was quickly rescinded after vehement protests from Portugal, widespread domestic criticism of the measure, and legal opinions that the regulation was illegal since it violated France's treaty commitment.[20] German bilateral treaties similarly were uneven in family-entry provisions. German treaties with Spain, Greece, and Portugal contained provisions for family entry, while treaties with Turkey, Morocco, and Yugoslavia did not.[21]

Most of the bilateral manpower treaties were valid for one or two years, but some were valid for longer periods. The Franco-Tunisian and Franco-Moroccan treaties of 1963, for example, were valid for ten and five years, respectively.[22] In practice, however, the formal time limitations of treaties were of little importance because they were renewed by tacit consent in all cases upon expiration until 1973, when Algeria unilaterally suspended further labor emigration to France. In 1973-1974 all Western European states unilaterally suspended recruitment without prior consultation of their labor partners, although some bilateral agreements called for notice to be given of suspension.

The unilateral nature of the decisions to halt labor recruitment testified to the essentially unequal nature of Western European bilateral labor agreements signed in the 1960s. As Maurice Flory, one of the leading European experts on bilateral manpower treaties has concluded, the treaties were primarily written to ensure the provision of sufficient quantities of foreigners who were young, healthy, and capable of doing often-difficult work.[23] The interests of the foreign workers and their native societies were poorly protected because most treaties did not contain concrete, detailed provisions for foreign-worker vocational training, adequate living conditions, socioeconomic rights, and so on. These lacunae have been partially compensated for by the various instruments proposed by international organizations and by unilateral action on the part of host governments, sometimes under the pressure of domestic or international criticism. However, the deficiencies and inequalities that characterized bilateral labor accords are at least partially responsible for the disfavored status of many foreign workers and their dependents at present.

The Franco-Algerian Case

Among Western European bilateral labor agreements, the Franco-Algerian migrant-labor program is of particular interest because of certain similarities with the U.S.-Mexican relationship in migrant matters and because the Franco-Algerian experience indicates the importance that bilateral labor agreements can assume in foreign relations generally. While the Franco-Algerian case in many ways is not typical of the diplomacy surrounding other bilateral labor programs in Western Europe, it does underscore several of the shortcomings characterized by Western European bilateral labor treaties in general, and it suggests the negative effects that bilateral foreign-worker programs can have upon overall diplomatic relations.

In comparative terms, both Mexico and Algeria are relatively poor developing countries with important energy resources, high rates of population growth, and massive unemployment. Both countries have played influential roles within the third world bloc. For France and the United States, respectively, Algeria and Mexico are key diplomatic concerns—Algeria because of its regional influence in the Arab world and Mexico for its influence in Latin America and the Caribbean. Furthermore, deep and often painful historical ties link the nations. In both cases, a special diplomatic relationship can be said to prevail despite historical grievances on the part of the labor-exporting state and a gulf in mutual comprehension stemming from cultural differences along with volatile sensitivity (even mutual antagonism) in the face of bilateral differences. The Franco-Algerian and U.S.-Mexican cases are examples of migrant labor relationships that are inextricably linked to the tone and context of overall bilateral relations.[24]

The historical background of Franco-Algerian ties, unlike the U.S.-Mexican case, is one of direct colonial domination. Prior to independence in 1962, after eight years of insurrection, Algeria was considered an integral part of France. In 1947, as part of a belated effort to integrate increasingly nationalistic and resentful Algerian Muslims, barriers to Algerian emigration to mainland France were removed. The result was large-scale labor emigration to the mainland, a flow that accelerated in 1954 with the outbreak of guerrilla warfare. By 1962, some 300,000 Algerian Muslims lived in mainland France. Under the terms of the Evian Accords recognizing Algeria's right to declare independence, Algerian Muslims could choose French or Algerian citizenship. Most chose Algerian citizenship. Algerians living in France were free to remain there because the Evian Accords included a provision for freedom of movement between the two countries.

In part due to French feeling that the massive repatriation of Pied Noirs (French citizens living in Algeria) had rendered inoperative the freedom-of-circulation provision, but also because tens of thousands of Algerian nationals were emigrating to France due to the disastrous state of the Algerian economy, France quickly insisted upon renegotiation of the Evian Accords. As table 4-1 indicates, well over 100,000 Algerians emigrated to France in the 1962-1964 period.

In 1964, the French efforts to rationalize Algerian emigration met with limited success. Algeria agreed to an annual quota of 12,000 new emigrant workers, but the privileged status of these emigrants vis-à-vis other migrant groups was reaffirmed. (See appendix H.) Algeria controlled the recruitment of the annual contingents, and Algerian emigrants were not subject to the formal restrictions governing the entry of most other nationality groups. They could, for example, look for work in France and were not limited to one occupation or region, and, when they found work, they were given ten-year residency permits. The privileged status of Algerian workers was more formal than real, however, as most foreign workers in the 1960s also could look for work in France and then have their status legalized. With the traumas of colonization and warfare still fresh, the 1964 decision to permit further emigration was a difficult but pragmatic choice for the Algerian leadership. Continued emigration could only be justified as a temporary measure within an overall policy of return.[25]

Algerian dissatisfaction with the de facto erosion of its privileged labor relationship with France, especially relative to the Portuguese, the new importance attached to France's politique arabe in the aftermath of the 1967 Arab-Israeli war, and growing French manpower needs combined to strengthen Algeria's bargaining position when the Franco-Algerian labor program was renegotiated in 1968. Under the terms of the treaty signed in that year, the annual quota was increased to 25,000 to 35,000, and France promised to improve housing conditions, vocational training opportunities, and public protection of Algerian emigrants.

Sporadic attacks upon Algerians living in France, poor housing, especially in the shantytowns that sprang up around French urban centers in the 1960s, and the lack of training opportunities for migrant workers were a source of concern for Algerian authorities by 1968. Despite some progress in housing matters, the situation of Algerian migrants in France, if anything, deteriorated in the following years. Algerian nationalization of French oil interests led to an outpouring of anti-Algerian sentiment and to a series of attacks on Algerian citizens living in France. These incidents had a deleterious effect on overall Franco-Algerian relations, culminating in the unilateral Algerian decision in August 1973 to halt further labor emigration.

During the period 1973-1979, overall Franco-Algerian relations worsened, and unresolved issues concerning migrant workers played a major role in the diplomatic falling out. As integration problems associated with foreign workers in general but Algerians in particular grew and the French

Table 4-1
Evolution of Algerian Emigration to France, 1961-1979

Year	Departures from Algeria	Returning to Algeria	Migration Balance	Algerians in France
1961	132,201	128,755	+ 5,455	
1962	180,167	155,018	+25,149	350,484
1963	262,075	211,532	+50,543	(census)
1964	269,543	225,741	+43,802	
1965	228,093	237,374	− 9,281	
1966	256,000	220,432	+35,568	
1967	209,867	198,301	+11,566	
1968	230,920	198,165	+32,755	530,000
1969	257,647	230,319	+27,328	
1970	352,530	291,408	+61,112	
1971	409,316	372,476	+36,840	
1972	409,146	385,372	+23,774	800,000
1973			+19,142	
1974	549,889	541,767	+ 8,122	
1975	592,458	595,986	− 3,528	884,000[a]

Sources: *News from France* (French Embassy), January 16, 1977, p. 28; Ministère du Travail, *Premiers éléments statistiques sur l'immigration en France en 1975,* (Paris, 1976), p. 16; "Regards sur l'actualité," (French embassy press release), January 1979; Mark Miller, "Reluctant Partnership: Foreign Workers in Franco-Algerian Relations, 1962-1979," *Journal of International Affairs* 33 (1979:229). Reprinted with permission.

[a]As of January 1979.

economy entered into a long period of recession, the French government pressed its effort to normalize the status of Algerians and to reduce the Algerian population living in France. The nadir in Franco-Algerian relations was reached in 1977-1978 when the French government threatened not to renew some 300,000 Algerian visas that were due to expire and French warplanes attacked Algerian-backed Polisario guerrillas in Mauritania. Only the death of Algerian President Houari Boumédienne in late 1978 enabled long-suspended bilateral negotiations on migrant questions to resume.

Conciliatory measures by both governments, including the temporary renewal of Algerian visas, could not conceal the continuing gulf between the two governments' viewpoints on Algerian migrant-labor questions, even though other aspects of bilateral relations showed remarkable improvement in late 1979 and early 1980. Indeed, differences over migrant workers were seen as the major stumbling block to Franco-Algerian entente. The French government steadfastly insisted upon normalization of the Algerian emigrant-worker status and implementation of Algeria's long-standing policy of return. Algeria insisted upon French recognition of the principle of voluntary repatriation and maintained that French failure to provide training opportunities prevented the return of Algerian workers.

The difficulties encountered in bilateral negotiations caused the French foreign minister Jean François-Poncet to postpone his planned trip to Algiers during the summer of 1980. Then in September, after negotiations between François-Poncet and his Algerian counterpart, a compromise agreement on foreign-labor issues was announced. To Algeria's satisfaction, the French agreed to recognize the principle of voluntary return and to renew some 400,000 visas for three years and three months, thereby reducing the insecurity felt by the Algerian community in France.

While recognizing the principle of voluntary return, however, the two governments agreed to undertake a coordinated effort to encourage returns. To this end, a return bonus equal to four months' salary or the opportunity to participate in a two- to eight-month vocational training program was promised. France agreed to spend 700 million francs ($130 million) to build vocational training facilities in Algeria, and the Algerian government undertook to grant fiscal and customs duty advantages to emigrant workers who return home permanently and to grant them access to new housing, financed in part with French loans. French representatives announced that starting in 1983, they expected 35,000 Algerians to return home annually as a result of the agreement.

The French minister in charge of migrant-work matters, Lionel Stoleru, hailed the Franco-Algerian accords of 1980 as "an historic moment in the North-South dialogue":

> They are stunning proof that the return of migrant workers can be a subject of cooperation, and not of dispute, between nations. . . . We hope that other nations will be inspired by this example to sign similar accords with France.[26]

Many observers, however, were less sanguine than Stoleru. Fewer than 2,500 Algerians had returned home under the cash bonus system instituted in 1977, and a bonus equivalent to four months' salary would not provide much more of an incentive than the 10,000 francs offered previously. There also was skepticism as to vocational training incentives, which also had been promised in 1968. The 700 million francs provided by the Fonds d'action sociale, itself financed in large part by savings realized by making lower child-support payments to foreign-worker children still in their home countries, were seen as inadequate to finance the return goals. The accords also did not resolve the troublesome question of the nationality of 300,000 Algerian children born on French soil.[27]

While the 1980 accords certainly marked a forward step in overall Franco-Algerian relations, the difficulties encountered in bilateral negotiations on migrant workers and the skepticism that greeted the announcement of the accords indicate that foreign-worker issues will remain an important source of strain in the Franco-Algerian special relationship. Since 1962, migrant-worker issues either have contributed to the deterioration of Franco-Algerian relations or have impeded their improvement. In the next few years, international attention will be focused on the Franco-Algerian model of organized return. This factor alone may stimulate positive results, but the past history of the Franco-Algerian migrant labor program cautions against excessive optimism.

The 1975 ILO Instruments and Other Diplomatic Influences

The tremendous growth and changed circumstances of migrant-labor populations in Western Europe and elsewhere in the world over the quarter-century following the adoption of convention 97 and recommendation 86 prompted reexamination of migrant-labor standards by the 1974 and 1975 ILO conferences. (See appendix B.) This reappraisal culminated in the adoption of convention 143 and recommendation 151. Convention 143 contains two parts concerning migrant workers in abusive conditions and equality of migrant treatment and opportunity. Part I prescribes international norms applicable to illegal aliens or migrants "submitted to conditions contravening pertinent international, multilateral and bilateral instruments and accords or national legislation."[28] It includes provisions aimed at stopping illegal migration through legal action against organizers of clandestine entry and employers of illegal aliens. Concomitantly, it proposes minimal legal protections for illegal aliens and recognition of their fundamental human rights. Concerning deportation and expulsion, the convention proposes that illegal aliens have suspensive appeal rights and that they have access to legal aid and translators.

Part II of convention 143, based upon convention 111 concerning employment and occupational discrimination, basically reaffirms the equality of migrant-worker rights and treatment in trade union, social security, and cultural matters.[29] It does permit restrictions on the quality of access to employment. In other words, signature of part II would not preclude giving priority to indigenous workers. The three-part recommendation 151 that accompanied convention 143 outlines an equitable social policy toward migrant workers. Most notably, measures pertaining to family reunification and migrant-worker rights in the event of loss of employment are suggested.

Convention 143 came into force in December 1978 and, as of March 1980, only eight states had ratified it entirely or in part. None of the Western European states under consideration here ratified it. However, France, Switzerland, and Germany each have taken stiffer stands against traffickers and employers of illegal aliens, a development due to internal economic conditions and convention 143. One reason why the effects of ILO instruments on foreign-worker policies are difficult to ascertain is the profusion of governmental and nongovernmental international and regional organizations that have passed resolutions or proposed guidelines concerning migrant workers, especially in recent years.

The far-reaching provisions of the United Nation's Universal Declaration of Human Rights adopted in 1948, especially articles, 13, 16, 22, 23, and 25 concerning freedom of circulation, family rights, social security, work rights, and the right to decent living conditions, respectively, are of general pertinence to migrant workers. More recently, though, the United Nations has undertaken specific action relative to migrants. The Economic and Social Council's (ECOSOC) Resolution 1706 LIII, the General Assembly's Resolution 2920 XXVII, and the Human Rights Commission with Resolution 3 XXIX all condemned the illicit trafficking of migrant workers. During its thirty-second session in 1977, the U.N. General Assembly adopted a far-ranging resolution on measures designed to ameliorate the situation of migrant workers and respect for their human rights and dignity. This resolution, not binding on U.N. members, expressed the sense of previous resolutions, along with the concerns of UNESCO and the ILO. Its most notable provisions concern informing public opinion on the role of migrants in host societies, the problems of return and reintegration, the elimination of discrimination, and family reunification. The resolution also calls upon member states to ratify ILO Convention 143.[30]

Through UNESCO, the United Nations Conference on Trade and Development (UNCTAD), and the Subcommittee for the Prevention of Discrimination and Protection of Minorities, the United Nations has attached growing attention to migrant-worker questions and thereby has exerted a certain pressure in favor of migrant workers. While U.N. instruments concerning migrant workers primarily consist of nonbinding resolutions, these instruments help establish international norms for the treatment of migrant workers, which Western European and other states cannot disregard. The Economic and Social Council currently is considering a draft resolution, "Measures to Improve the Situation and Ensure the Human Rights and Dignity of all Migrant Workers," which counts Algeria and Mexico among its sponsors.

Among other governmental and nongovernmental international organizations that have influenced the evolution of Western European foreign-worker policies, the Inter-governmental Commission on European Migrations, the World Council of Churches, and the International Catholic Migration Commission are the most important. The two religious organizations generally have adopted resolutions and guidelines consonant with ILO and Council of Europe instruments concerning migrant workers and thereby have increased pressure for French, Swiss, or German policy reform because of the political clout of WCC and ICMC affiliates in the three countries.

Summary

Recognition of the important role played by international religious organizations in shaping the diplomatic context of Western European foreign-worker programs underscores four major points. The diplomatic underpinnings of such policies cannot be understood out of context of more general international events, foreign-worker programs do not take place in diplomatic-political voids. Second, international norms concerning foreign workers have tended to ameliorate the rights and socioeconomic conditions of Western European foreign workers. Third, the transnational influence of international organizations has tended to homogenize Western European policies toward foreign workers. Finally, international norms and expectations concerning foreign workers have been considerably modified by Western Europe's postwar experience; a fact that countries outside of Western Europe considering authorization of foreign-labor programs should not ignore. (Appendix H contains selected excerpts from international conventions and recommendations pertaining to foreign workers in Western Europe as adapted from an International Catholic Migration Commission document.)

Notes

1. *International Labor Standards* (Geneva: ILO, 1978), p. 53.

2. Paul Lewis, "The OECD Is a Reactor Now, Not an Initiator," *New York Times,* November 30, 1980, p. F22.

3. Charles Leben, "Le droit international et les migrations des travailleurs" in Société française pour le droit international, ed., *Les travailleurs étrangers et le droit international* (Paris: A. Pedone, 1979), pp. 59-60.

4. G. Rellini, "Les politiques de retour" in Société française pour le droit international, *Les travailleurs étrangers,* pp. 155-158.

5. *Manual of the Council of Europe* (London: Stevens and Sons, 1970), p. 11.

6. Herbert Golsong, "La convention européènne relative au statut juridique du travailleur migrant," in Société française pour le droit international, *Les travailleurs étrangers,* p. 233.

7. "Council of Europe Adopts a European Convention on the Legal Status of Migrant Workers," *Migration Today* 21 (1977):150-151.

8. Golsong, "La convention européenne," pp. 229-230.

9. Ray C. Rist, "The European Economic Community (EEC) and Manpower Migrations: Policies and Prospects," *Journal of International Affairs* 33 (1979):201.

10. Leben, "Le droit international," p. 67.

11. Rist, "The European Economic Community," pp. 207-210.

12. Ibid., p. 213.

13. Jacques Picard, "Les conventions bilatérales passés par la france," in Société française pour le droit international, *Les travailleurs* étrangers," p. 109.

14. Ibid., p. 110.

15. Jacques Barou, "Rôle des cultures d'originc ct adaptation des travailleurs africains en europe," in P. Bernard, ed., *Les travailleurs étrangers en europe occidentale* (Paris: Mouton, 1976), p. 230.

16. Picard, "Les conventions bilatérales passés par la france," pp. 110-111.

17. Leben, "Le droit international," p. 90.

18. Maurice Flory, "Orders juridiques et statut des travailleurs étrangers," in Société française pour le droit international, *Les travailleurs étrangers,* pp. 186-187.

19. Leben, "Le droit international," p. 980.

20. "France Drops Its Plan to Bar Families of Immigrants," *New York Times,* October 30, 1977.

21. Flory, "Orders juridiques," p. 187.

22. Leben, "Le droit international," p. 90.

23. Flory, "Orders juridiques," pp. 186-187.

24. For more detail, see Mark Miller, "Reluctant Partnership: Foreign Workers in Franco-Algerian Relations, 1962-1979," *Journal of International Affairs* 33 (1979):219-237. Reprinted with permission.

25. Stephen Adler, *International Migration and Dependence* (Hampshire, England: Saxon House, 1977) pp. 154-155.

26. Quoted in *Presse et immigrés en france,* no. 12, September 18-24, 1980, p. 3.

27. Daniel Junqua, "Paris et alger expériment leur satisfaction devant l'ampleur du contentieux apuré," *Le monde,* September 20, 1980.

28. See J.H. Laserre-Bigory, "Reglementations internationales concernant les migrations clandestines," in Société française pour le droit internationale, *Les travailleurs étrangers,* pp. 129-137.

29. ILO Committee of Experts, *Migrant Workers* (Geneva:ILO, 1980), p. 6.

30. Flory, "Orders juridiques," pp. 194-195.

5   # Recruitment
Procedures

Labor-receiving countries have three options concerning the administration of foreign-worker recruitment. Most often, the government organizes recruitment in conjunction with labor officials from out-migration countries. However, the homeland may also be permitted to select and transport a quota of workers, who are then granted work and residency rights upon finding a job. The third option is to permit host-nation employers to recruit foreign workers directly.

France and Germany gave a recruitment monopoly to a governmental organ, the National Immigration Office (*Office national d'immigration*) and the Federal Labor Agency (*Bundesanstalt Für Arbeit*), respectively. The ONI is a specialized agency dealing exclusively with immigration matters under the supervision of the Ministry of Labor and Participation. The Federal Labor Agency is responsible for the administration of all labor-related matters in Germany. Hence foreign-labor recruitment falls within the purview of its mission. Legally, then, French and German employers cannot contract with alien workers outside of the procedures laid down by these two governmental agencies, although some German foreign workers were able to enter with visas and look for work until 1972, and the status of undocumented workers in France long was readily legalized after they found jobs. Privileged categories of workers such as Algerian workers in France and EEC workers are excluded from normal procedures.

The Swiss, on the other hand, allow employers to contract directly with foreign workers as long as Swiss and labor-source-country regulations are respected. The contract is then submitted for residency-work authorization to cantonal labor offices. Once approved, a recommendation is made to the Swiss Justice Department's Aliens Police that the worker be granted a residency permit.[1] If a worker is abroad, the worker receives an assurance document entitling that person to residency authorization upon arrival in Switzerland. Swiss employer associations help individual employers locate suitable workers abroad.

Employer Requests

The recruitment process begins with employer requests for foreign workers. In all three countries, labor ministry officials must concur that indigenous workers cannot be found and that foreign-worker recruitment will not have an adverse effect on wages and working conditions. Such labor-market tests were largely pro forma until 1973. In France and Germany, notice of an unfilled job offer was sent to the EEC's labor exchange first. If the job remained unfilled for two weeks after notification of the EEC, notice was sent to non-EEC countries. Generally employer requests for non-EEC foreign workers were approved for transmittal to government-run recruitment offices abroad after a month's delay. However, during the peak recruitment years, German employer requests sometimes were sent abroad much more quickly. Conversely, the slowness of the ONI's recruitment proceedings in the early 1960s encouraged French employers to hire illegal aliens on the spot.

There are two kinds of employer requests: anonymous and nominative. Anonymous requests, the more prevalent of the two, specify desired skills and work qualities, including national background, but leave the selection of the individual migrant up to recruitment officials. Nominative requests ask for specific individuals known to the employer. Both kinds of requests were transmitted to recruitment offices abroad, so even nominative requests required at least nominal approval for emigration. However, nominative requests precluded any role for homeland officials in the selection of candidates for emigration.[2] Consequently, nominative requests tended to undercut the migrant selection strategies of emigrant-sending countries, which generally were aimed at the retention of skilled workers and the emigration of redundant and low-skilled workers. Also, individuals receiving nominative requests avoided waiting list delays although they still had to pass medical and character tests; for example, a convicted criminal would be barred from emigrating even if requested personally.

Homeland Government Role

Major emigrant-sending countries consented to recruitment of their workers through bilateral treaties, which specified the roles to be taken by the sending and receiving governments in the recruitment process. Additionally, however, most migrant-sending countries have emigration laws whose nature is highly variable, ranging from minimal measures to limit the outflow of skilled workers (as in Tunisia) to complex laws detailing emigrant rights and setting out conditions for employment abroad (as in Italy and Yugoslavia). Unlike other major emigration countries, Algeria would not permit foreign employers or Western European governments to recruit on its soil. The Algerian government administers the selection, orientation, and departure of its migrant workers to France through a specialized governmental agency, known by the acronym ONAMO. Other countries, such as Spain with its Instituto Español de Emigración, also have specialized governmental agencies concerned with emigration, but they nonetheless permit labor-receiving governments to organize worker recruitment. Bilateral cooperation is the norm for the Germans and the French. In most cases, this cooperation is between the ONI or the German Federal Labor Agency and the labor department of the migrant-sending nation.

Recruitment Bureau Systems

After employer requests were transmitted to ONI or Federal Labor Agency bureaus abroad, indigenous labor ministries or other appropriate authorities were informed of the requests and recommended individuals for the jobs in Europe. Most French and German recruitment bureaus were located in capitol cities and major population centers. Hence, these systems tended to be highly centralized, lowering administrative costs. Depending on the nature of the homeland labor ministries, the overall recruitment process could be decentralized or centralized. Yugoslav and Spanish labor ministries were examples of decentralized recruitment, while Turkish labor ministry recruitment was highly centralized. The advantages accruing to the Spaniards and Yugoslavs in comparison to the Turks were considerable. They were more able to avoid local labor shortages due to excessive emigration and to respond to regional labor imbalances, although the loss of skilled labor was an acute problem for Yugoslavia. Decentralization also spared aspiring emigrant workers the time and expense of long journeys to urban areas to apply for work abroad.

German and French recruitment bureaus were staffed by both Europeans and natives of the labor-sending countries. European labor officials held the more important posts. The salaries of personnel working in the ONI or Federal Labor Agency branches abroad were paid by the French and German governments. The fee paid by employers for foreign-worker recruitment partially offset this expense. Homeland labor ministry personnel involved in the screening of emigrant workers usually were paid by the labor-exporting governments.

Selection Criteria

Recruits for French and German jobs had to fulfill selection criteria pertaining to age, sex, health, vocational aptitude, family status, and character. Unmarried males between the ages of eighteen to forty with some education were the ideal candidates.

The major duty of homeland labor ministries in the recruitment process was to prescreen potential foreign workers and to notify them of job opportunities abroad. Homeland societies generally wanted to send unskilled workers, but many skilled workers became emigrants. Turkey and Yugoslavia both experienced significant losses of skilled workers to Germany.

In most cases, final determination of who would be given the opportunity to work in Western Europe was left to German and French recruitment authorities after homeland labor ministry authorities submitted the names and credentials of suitable candidates for job openings. These candidates would then complete a battery of medical, vocational, and character examinations.

Medical Examinations

Candidates for emigration were tested for their physical ability to perform certain jobs, as well as for their general health. Despite a significant rejection rate of aspiring foreign workers on health grounds, French, German, and Swiss medical examinations did not screen out many of the migrants who fell ill soon after arriving in Western Europe.[3] Future tuberculosis cases were especially difficult to detect. (Apparently healthy migrants fell prey to tuberculosis because of emotional stress occasioned by adaptation to life in the host societies.) The Swiss subject all foreign workers to a medical examination at their points of entry.

Vocational Tests

Employer requests for vocational skills were filled primarily by recruits with qualifications certified by the homeland labor ministries. However, recruits often were required to take additional aptitude and dexterity tests and would be assigned to jobs on that basis. Qualification standards in the homelands did not always suit employers who had contracted for skilled labor. A Tunisian mason, for example, had to undergo considerable on-the-job training in France to be brought up to French standards.

Character Tests

Foreign recruits were screened for criminal behavior and social or mental disorders. Convicted criminals generally were not allowed to emigrate. Nonetheless, notable members of foreign workers did suffer mental disorders or engaged in criminal activity in the host societies. Turkish drug smuggling in Germany is particularly prevalent. Again, this pointed to the difficulty of screening for behavior that could be largely associated with adaptation problems in the host society. While foreign-worker criminality may have slightly exceeded indigenous crime rates, it is important to note that newspapers frequently engage in sensationalistic reporting on alien crimes. Indeed, crime stories comprise a major category of press coverage given to migrant affairs.[4]

Priority Lists

Of all selection criteria, length of waiting time probably was the most important for unskilled workers because the sheer size of the pool of unskilled manpower eligible and willing to emigrate could mean that it would be years before individual migrants would get contracts. When Germany announced its recruitment ban in 1973, there were some 1.4 million workers on the Turkish waiting list alone. Long waiting lists increased the potential for corruption, which, in cases like Morocco, was endemic throughout the preselection process.[5] Long waiting lists also probably encouraged some workers to migrate illegally. Although it is impossible to prove, it seems plausible that workers who went through selection procedures but did not get work contracts in Western Europe are prime candidates for illegal emigration.

Preparation for Departure

Once an employer request was matched with a recruit, a contract, usually translated for the migrant, was signed. Wages, hours, vacations, insurance, and housing provisions were stipulated by governmental officials. Wages were set in accordance with prevailing wages as determined by industry wage agreements between employers and unions or by labor ministry monitoring of average wages for a trade. A migrant who broke a contract before one year was completed would risk having his or her residency rights revoked. Signature of a contract approved by the ONI or the Federal Labor Agency guaranteed initial residency and work permits, which later could be renewed. Visas were granted to the workers at no cost. Recruits then were given predeparture orientation wherein they were advised of their rights and acquainted with host-society institutions and customs. Most migrants were given free transportation to their destinations; this expense was part of the fee assessed employers for hiring foreign workers. In Switzerland employers reimbursed foreign workers or the Italian government for transportation expenses. Emigrant workers also were accorded special customs considerations.

Reception Services

The French, German, and Swiss governments each subsidized semigovernmental and private (largely church-affiliated) organizations to counsel foreign workers upon arrival. These reception services were organized into nationwide networks of bureaus where foreign workers could find translators, legal assistance, help in finding housing, information concerning the host country, intensive language courses in French or German, and personal counseling. In principle, these services were to be provided free of charge. The reception services of the three countries improved with time but especially after serious integration problems had become apparent. Many of these centers now employ alien social workers, and their personnel undergo special training to prepare them for the problems encountered by migrants in Western Europe. Nonetheless, many newly arrived workers experience severe adaptation problems.[6]

Employer Fees

The administrative costs of foreign-worker recruitment are partially offset by special taxes assessed employers of alien labor. In Germany, the fee paid for each foreign worker recruited was raised from 350 DM prior to 1973 to 1,000 DM ($430) at present.[7] In France, the fee was raised from 500 FF ($125) prior to 1975 to 1,500 FF ($375).[8] Fees are lower if aliens are hired for domestic help or seasonal agricultural work in France. Switzerland has a complex system of fees for residency permits and other administrative documents necessary to foreign workers. In principle, these fees are paid by Swiss employers.

The French and Germans used the fee increases to discourage employer recourse to foreign workers, but still it often was cheaper for employers to hire foreign workers than it was to hire indigenous workers despite regulations requiring equal pay for foreign and indigenous workers. Foreign workers sometimes were assigned to jobs with low skill ratings and correspondingly low wages even if their work was essentially the same done by indigenous workers with higher ratings. This discrepancy prompted several foreign-worker strikes in the early 1970s.[9] In his 1976 study of alien construction workers near Grenoble, France, for example, R.E. Verhaeren found systematic wage discrepancies between French and foreign workers, due to employers withholding bonuses usually paid to French workers and paying aliens at rates that did not correspond to prevailing wages for the type of work done.

Policies against Illegal Immigration

A component of any foreign-worker recruitment system is a series of legal penalties for violations of recruitment procedures. Detection of illegal-alien employment in the three Western European countries under consideration is facilitated by the requirement that all citizens have identity papers. Legally introduced foreign workers must always carry their residency and/or work permits. Nonetheless, there has been a significant problem with illegal aliens in Western Europe. In France, the illegal-alien population is estimated at between 300,000 and 500,000.[10] In Germany it is put between 200,000 and 500,000.[11] These figures represent between 5 and 15 percent of the total legally resident alien populations in the two countries.

Illegal aliens in Western Europe include individuals who have entered outside of recruitment procedures, those who were entitled to legal residency but have overstayed their permits, those who have valid residency permits but have taken up employment illegally, and those who possess work permits but have abused them by working at unauthorized jobs.[12] A final category of illegal aliens includes those who have migrated without documents and then have taken up employment. These migrants often are smuggled in.

**Present Patterns of Illegal-Alien Flows
to Western Europe**

Contemporary inflows of illegal aliens characteristically are from countries geographically removed from Western Europe. Citizens of India, Pakistan, and the Philippines along with black Africans and citizens of Middle Eastern countries seem to comprise the majority of recent illegal entrants. Their means of entry are varied. Pakistanis often fly to East Berlin and then take jobs in West Berlin. Indian and Pakistani citizens also might fly to Belgium and then clandestinely enter France by truck through lightly controlled border posts. Africans often illegally enter France by way of the physically dangerous route once taken by many Portuguese migrants: the Pyrenees. They also reach France by stowing away on ships or by land routes through Italy and Switzerland. In all of these cases, illegal entry tends to be abetted by traffickers who often receive considerable sums of money from their illegal-alien clients and in some cases also from employers. Illegal migrants often use all or much of their personal or family savings to pay transportation and smuggling fees.

In addition to illegal entrants, Western European states must contend with visa abusers, overstayers, and residents who take jobs without permission. In the first case, Western European states have taken measures to restrict the granting of visas. In the second case, internal controls have been reinforced either through spot checks or centralized computer record keeping. The third case is more difficult to control because the dependents of foreign workers with residency rights often take jobs, a situation that is extremely difficult to monitor. For example, it is virtually impossible to detect a foreign-worker spouse who has taken part-time employment as a housekeeper.

Penalties

Western Europe laws against illegal immigration focus on traffickers and employers. Traffickers in France are subject to fines and prison sentences up to $50,000 and two years in prison.[13] German employers convicted of knowingly hiring illegally introduced aliens or keeping foreign workers who have overstayed their permits face three to five years in jail and/or fines of up to 50,000 DM ($20,000).[14] French employers face fines of up to $600.[15] Swiss employers also face jail terms and must pay the repatriation and other costs of removing illegal workers. European employers must submit their employment records for examination if so notified. In all three countries, employers of illegal aliens, if detected, lose the right to hire foreign workers permanently or for a period of several years and retroactively must pay social security taxes for the illegal aliens. Illegal aliens themselves are subject to detention and deportation and are permanently barred from returning. Many illegal aliens, however, are simply released at the border without going through deportation hearings.[16]

In 1976, almost 10,000 German employers were fined for employing illegal aliens, and some 2,000 employers were fined in France in 1977.[17] Suppression of illicit-alien employment has become more difficult with the development of foreign-worker ghettoes, which provide havens for illegal aliens and are difficult for enforcement officials to penetrate.

Illegal-alien employment is a problem. In France, illegal aliens were long allowed to regularize or adjust their status, and this has undermined French efforts to gain control over the foreign-worker influx. Enforcement efforts have been stepped up since the economic recession of 1973, exposing governments to the charge that enforcement depends on the unemployment rate. Alleged government toleration of illegal-alien employment during a period of recession has given rise to protests against enforcement measures.

Notes

1. Office fedérale de l'industrie, des arts et métiers et du travail, *Directives et commentaires* (Bern: OFIAMT, October 25, 1976), pp. 81-89.

2. Abdellah Boudahrain, "Regime international des travailleurs migrants marocains (Ph.D. diss., University of Paris-I, 1978), pp. 95-96.

3. Stephen Castles and Godula Kosack, *Immigrant Workers and Class Structure in Western Europe* (London: University of Oxford Press, 1973), pp. 318-325.

4. J.M. Delgado, *Die Gastarbeiter in der Presse* (Opladen: 1972).

5. Boudahrain, "Regime international," p. 124.

6. P. Bernard, ed., *Les travailleurs étrangers in europe occidentale* (Paris: Mouton, 1976), pp. 163-318.

7. Inter Nationes (German government publication), *Social Report*, February 1978, p. 10.

8. *Le monde*, March 23, 1978.

9. Eckart Hildebrandt and Werner Olle, *Ihr Kampf ist unser Kampf-Ursachen, Verlauf und Perspektiven der Ausländerstriks 1973 in der BRD* (Offenback: Verlag 2000, 1975), pp. 99-104.

10. Catherine Wihtol de Wenden, "Undocumented Workers in France" (unpublished paper, 1980), p. 3.

11. See *Rundschau* (Carl Schurz Association), May 1975, p. 4, *Washington Post*, October 31, 1974, and *German Tribune*, March 7, 1974.

12. de Wenden, "Undocumented Workers in France," pp. 1-2.

13. *Le monde*, April 19, June 15, 1979.

14. Inter Nationes, *Social Report*, February 1975.

15. David North, "Foreign Workers: Unwanted Guests," *Transatlantic Perspectives* 1 (1979):20.

16. *Le monde*, April 24, 1979.

17. D. North, "Foreign Workers: Unwanted Guests," p. 20.

6

Employment-Related Rights

Western European trade unions, with the help of pro-labor political parties, church groups, and diplomatic influences, have been increasingly successful in securing equality of employment-related rights between indigenous and foreign workers. Trade-union support for equality of rights stems not only from traditional solidarity but also from pragmatic considerations. By giving foreign workers equal rights, prevailing wages and working conditions are less likely to be undercut. Also alien workers can be organized into unions more readily, if they enjoy normal labor rights.

In the three countries under consideration, major trade unions insisted upon equality of employment-related rights from the outset of postwar foreign-labor recruitment. Although the unions usually favored more-restrictive migration policies throughout the postwar period, their opposition to large-scale migration policies should not be confused with putative opposition or hostility to migrant workers. Once a migrant worker is in the country, Western European unions favor equality of rights for the individual. In France, this attitude extends even to certain categories of illegal aliens.

The major exception to equality of employment-related rights stems from the discrimination inherent in any temporary alien-worker policy: the question of the function and renewal of work and residency permits. However, even this fundamental difference between foreign and citizen workers eventually was mitigated by national and international policies that rejected the forcible repatriation of employed and unemployed foreign workers. While an estimated 2 million or almost one-third of all foreign workers did leave Western Europe between 1973 and 1978, most of those returning left of their own volition. Most returnees seem to have left because of worsening economic prospects and the sociopolitical malaise caused by the recession rather than because of nonrenewal or loss of work and residency authorization.[1] Most foreign workers have not left Western Europe despite high unemployment, however. The bilateral and multilateral diplomatic commitments and domestic and international pressures against rotation or forced repatriation policies have made the Western European migrant-worker policies (with the exception of French and Swiss seasonal-worker programs) de facto immigraton policies.

Work and Residency Permit Insecurity

Reductions in the numbers of employed foreigners since 1973 are explained by the continuing outflow of returnees while recruitment has stopped. Administrative withdrawal of work and residency authorization is the exception rather than the rule. However, because the work and residency permit systems require foreign workers to renew their permits, the status of these workers must be regarded as contingent. If the three governments under consideration have generally adhered to their declared policies against nonvoluntary repatriation, it also is true that a climate of insecurity surrounds the sojourn of many foreign workers.[2]

Since 1973, renewal of work and residency permits, formerly a quasi-automatic process, has become more difficult. For example, native workers, including privileged foreign workers, are given preference over a foreigner if both apply for the same job, although this does not mean that an indigenous worker can bump a foreigner from his or her job. Also, this priority given to indigenous labor enters into decisions to renew permits for short-term workers—nonprivileged workers usually with fewer than five years of residency. At present, fewer than a quarter of all foreign workers fall into this short-term category, and job holders' permits almost always are renewed. The most vulnerable group are unemployed foreigners. If they have been out of work for six months to a year and their permits come up for renewal, they can be denied renewal and be ordered to leave the country on the grounds that they are public charges or "burdens." There are no statistics on how many unemployed foreigners have been denied permit renewal and thereby are forced to repatriate, but the number is small relative to the declines registered in foreign-worker employment levels.

Although relatively few foreign workers are denied permit renewal, they remain insecure about their status because of the not-infrequent calls to reduce foreign populations. They also worry about losing their work and residency permits. Administrative errors and shortcomings can occur, especially since French and German foreign workers must keep their papers in order with two distinct administrations. The apprehension the foreign workers feel about their work and residency permit renewal contributes to the syndrome of poor housing, migrant isolation, and feelings of inferiority, and resentment vis-à-vis indigenous workers. In the housing area, for example, insecurity accentuates the tendency of migrants to accept substandard living conditions so as to maximize savings, because migrants fear that they may be forced to return home before realizing the economic objectives which motivated their emigration in the first place.

Frequently it has been charged that the insecurity created by limited work and residency permits has fostered foreign-worker docility in the face of normally unacceptable working conditions. To a certain extent, this was true, especially in the early years of postwar migration. However, the same factors that initially fostered docility eventually gave rise to resentment and militancy. As foreign workers became more conscious of their considerable labor and social rights, they became less docile. Particularly in France, where work and residency authorization sometimes is withdrawn on the grounds that individuals, mainly political activists, have disturbed the public order, protest movements have developed to overturn decisions denying permit renewal.

Union Rights

Foreign workers in Western Europe are free to join existing unions, and their membership is encouraged by the unions. The right to union membership is granted on the basis of host-society law and often is included in bilateral treaties as well. Foreign workers can create their own autonomous unions, but no significant such unions exist. In France, an autonomous union as an association of aliens would require special police authorization which would likely prove difficult to obtain because French employers and unions would oppose it. There are, however, significant foreign-worker cultural and national associations, which affiliate with or encourage their members to join existing unions and thus exert a somewhat autonomous influence in union affairs. These include the 60,000-member Amicale des algériens en europe (AAE) in France and the Federazione Colonie Libere Italiane (FCLI) and Association des travailleurs émigrés espagnols en suisse (ATEES) with 15,000 and 5,000 members, respectively, in Switzerland.

Foreign-worker participation in unions reflects prevailing unionization patterns in the respective host countries. The overall unionization rate in Germany is comparatively high (around 40 percent) and so is that of guest workers (around 35 percent). Estimates of foreign-worker unionization rates in Switzerland and France are 20 and 10 to 15 percent, respectively, compared to 30 and 23 percent for the two work forces as a whole. Among foreign-worker nationality groups, unionization rates vary considerably. Turks in Germany, for example, unionize at a rate of 47 percent, considerably higher than other nationality groups.[3] In France, according to trade-union sources, Algerians unionize much more readily than do Portuguese workers. Overall foreign-worker unionization correlates with residency duration, and all indications are that the foreign-worker unionization rate will equal or exceed that of indigenous workers in the near future. In the German steelworking industry, the unionization rate of foreigners (52.7 percent) exceeded that of German workers (52.3 percent) by 1975.[4] In France, foreign-worker concentration in blue-collar jobs has resulted in large foreign-worker membership in some trade unions as a proportion of overall membership. This is true of the relatively weak French construction union affiliated with the Confédération Général du travail (CGT) and the Swiss construction union affiliate where foreign workers composed one-third of the total membership as early as 1961. Now foreigners represent three-quarters of the Swiss construction union membership.[5]

Western European unions have supported equal economic and, to a lesser extent, social rights for foreign workers since the advent of postwar immigration policies. Although unions deserve much of the credit for seeing that foreign workers got their rights, it would be inaccurate to say that the foreign worker-Western European trade union relationship has been easy or exemplary. The trade unions did not pay much attention to the specific needs of foreign workers until the late 1960s and early 1970s, and this inattention, at times exacerbated by the prejudices of some rank-and-file unionists, resulted in a certain foreign-worker disaffection from the unions, manifest in foreign-worker wildcat strikes with antiunion overtones. This situation began to change only as the numbers of foreign workers grew enormously in the late 1960s and as union leaderships realized the consequences of not integrating foreign workers into union structures. Consequently the union's indifference toward foreign workers gave way to union efforts to organize foreign workers and to articulate their specific interests.

One important area in which the unions began to exert pressure was in the realm of union rights and the elimination of legal limitations upon foreign union members. In 1972, all barriers to foreign-worker participation in German and French works-council elections were eliminated, with the exception that foreign candidates for such posts in France had to be able to read and write in French. In 1975, this condition was modified so that foreigners able to express themselves in French became eligible for election. Restrictions also ended on the election of foreigners to leadership positions within unions, except in France where non-EEC workers can be elected to a union post only after five years of residency, and the proportion of foreigners in the leadership of a union cannot exceed one-third.

As union members, foreign workers can vote in union elections and, except for the lingering French restrictions, can be elected to shop steward and union leadership positions. They also can vote for and be elected to works councils in all three countries. Especially in Germany, works councils have significant influence in determining work hours, production tempos, hiring, vacation times, disciplinary proceedings, layoffs, and other employment-related matters. French and Swiss systems of industrial democracy are much less developed, and their work councils correspondingly are less influential.

The growing importance of foreign workers in trade unions and union efforts to become more responsive to foreign workers has resulted in a significant increase in foreigners' being elected to union and works-council positions. While still underrepresented, foreign-worker stewards in Germany increased from 642 in 1967 to 2,487 in 1970 and 5,719 in 1973.[6] Currently, about 3 percent of Germany's 195,000 works council members are migrants.[7] French union sources report similar increases, although foreign workers there also remain underrepresented in works-council and union positions.

Despite the problem of continuing foreign-worker underrepresentation, Western European unions clearly are more responsive to the specific needs and problems of foreign workers today than they were a decade ago. Foreign members generally are allowed to form language groups which permit aliens to discuss and conduct union business in their native tongues, and to receive various kinds of special representation within union structures, especially at the national level. National union headquarters include foreign-worker affairs departments, which advise the leadership on foreign-worker problems, lobby in support of foreign-worker interests, publish foreign-language union documents, and coordinate local or nationwide demonstrations and strikes on foreign-worker issues. In contrast to the 1960s, trade unions emerged as staunch defenders of foreign-worker interests in the 1970s, an evolution facilitated by the recruitment bans of 1973-1974, which removed an often exaggerated fear of foreign workers that stemmed from union opposition to policies allowing large numbers of foreigners to enter. Also foreign-worker populations have become more stable and hence more likely to unionize.

The Right to Strike

Foreign workers are guaranteed the right to strike in France and Germany. In Switzerland, the right to strike is not guaranteed by law but in practice is granted to both Swiss and foreign workers. Bilateral treaty arrangements might also mention strike rights. However, an alien worker's right to strike has to be regarded as contingent or problematical because it is limited by an overriding consideration: aliens cannot disrupt the public order.

In France, local police and Interior Ministry officials have broad discretionary authority to determine whether foreign-worker strikes are disruptive of the public order. Foreign-worker strikes and plant occupations sometimes elicit police intervention, resulting in violence, arrests, and mass firings. Strike activity has been most prevalent in comparatively strike-prone France, where foreign workers are in the forefront of labor militancy. Several recent French strikes with important economic and political repercussions have involved primarily foreign workers.

In the well-functioning German social partnership system of industrywide contracts, strikes are not legal unless sufficient notice is given and certain grievance procedures are followed. As long as strikes are union authorized, foreign workers are seen as acting within the law. However, a considerable number of wildcat or spontaneous strikes (significant because of the virtual absence of such strikes prior to 1970) involving foreign workers in the early 1970s were declared illegal and disruptive of the social peace.[8] Many of these strikes ended in confrontations between the police, supported by nonstriking German trade unionists, and striking foreigners. It seems that many wildcat strikes, such as the Ford-Cologne strike of 1973, were directed against trade-union representatives as well as against employers.[9] Foreign-worker strike activity in Germany crested in 1973. It has declined in part because of trade-union efforts to integrate foreign workers.

Swiss industrial relations resemble the German case. The Swiss similarly considered foreign-worker strikes in the late 1960s and early 1970s as disruptive of the social peace, but foreign-worker participation in rare union-sponsored strikes is tolerated. Foreign-labor militancy still is perceived as a threat to Swiss social peace traditions, but fears of foreign-worker radicalization have subsided in recent years.[10]

The crystallization of long latent foreign-worker militancy in the 1970s is to be primarily explained by increasing lengths of stay, a growing consciousness among foreign workers of their disfavored socioeconomic status, strike-organizing efforts by extreme leftists, and, not the least, by the reinforcement of foreign-worker labor rights. Factors which foster foreign-worker passivity in the early stages of migration, such as low unionization rates, language and other integration problems, a lack of understanding of labor rights, and relative indifference to working conditions can spark exceptional militancy and strike activity as migrant work forces mature. The fact that European unions often ignored foreign-worker problems or failed to integrate alien workers adequately within union structures resulted in disruptive strikes that undercut union claims to represent labor and consequently damaged collective-bargaining institutions. Specific grievances held by foreign workers, such as racism and discrimination, in addition to their socially and economically disfavored general status, makes foreign workers prime candidates for labor militancy if they choose to stay on in the host society.

Labor Rights

As employees in the social welfare states of Western Europe, foreign workers contribute to and benefit from a panoply of work-related insurance programs. They also benefit from employee rights as stipulated by social partnership or collective-bargaining agreements and national labor codes.

Most foreign workers are employed in jobs covered by collective-bargaining agreements in Germany and Switzerland. These agreements set wages, hours, overtime pay, vacations, worker grievance and dismissal procedures, work breaks, and various employee amenities such as company-sponsored soccer clubs or Christmas bonuses. In France, where industry-wide collective bargaining is comparatively weak, article 3 of the civil code stipulates that foreign workers benefit from the forty-hour week and overtime pay provisions, weekly rest and holidays, supplementary pay for night work, paid vacations, supplementary vacation for births, marriage, or death in the family, and all work-safety and health provisions.

Violations of collective-bargaining agreements and minimal work standards do occur, especially with respect to foreign workers who may be unaware of their rights. Foreign workers in an industry covered by collective-bargaining agreements have rights and duties equal to those of indigenous workers, which explains why spontaneous strikes by foreign workers are often considered illegal. Appendix J summarizes the work-related rights of various categories of foreign-work permit holders from country to country.

Vacations

In France, all employees by law are entitled to a one-month vacation. Swiss and German vacation periods generally are shorter and are set in collective wage agreements. But foreign workers often want to return home for an extended vacation, and these differences can create conflict. Several foreign-worker strikes have stemmed from disciplinary measures taken against foreign workers who did not return in time from vacations. And indigenous workers have complained of being laid off or forced to take vacations because the large number of foreign workers who leave for holidays disrupts production and forces factories to shut down. Extended vacations by foreign workers have also jeopardized their status as being continuously resident in a host society, which in turn affects work and residency permit renewal. Foreign-worker integration into unions and works councils in recent years, however, has promoted more accommodation to migrant needs. Muslim workers, especially, are likely to be granted their religious holidays.

Unemployment Compensation

Laid-off foreign workers in all three countries receive normal unemployment benefits, usually for one year. After that, foreign workers do not have a right to welfare benefits, but such benefits generally are extended to them on humanitarian grounds. Unemployed foreigners can eventually lose their residency permits. France encourages its 100,000 unemployed foreigners to repatriate with the *aide au retour* departure bonus program. Some German companies, particularly automobile manufacturers, give laid-off foreigners severance bonuses in the hope of inducing returns home. In 1980, unemployed foreigners in Germany had an unemployment rate of 11 percent as compared to 4.5 percent for the German work force.[11] Migrant unemployment rates are usually higher than rates for natives because migrants are concentrated in recession-sensitive industries like construction.

Vocational Training

Jobless foreigners in all three countries are eligible for vocational reorientation and training programs. Similarly foreign employees can participate in vocational-training programs designed to promote professional advancement. Indeed such training opportunities may be required by bilateral treaties. But despite formal access to such programs, foreign workers have complained of a lack of vocational-training opportunities. Often, for example, they encounter language barriers, which hold them back.

Most reports concur that relatively few foreign workers are benefiting from vocational-training opportunities. In France, for example, only 1 percent of all eligible foreign workers had benefited from vocational training as opposed to the 12.5 percent rate for indigenous workers by 1975.[12] Reasons given for the low rate of foreign participation included inadequate public funding, lack of specially trained instructors, and poor overall administration. Foreign workers frequently complain that the physically taxing nature of their jobs leaves them too exhausted to attend night classes.

Under considerable domestic and international pressure, all three governments have expanded vocational-training programs for foreign workers in recent years as a means of forestalling the development of a foreign-worker subproletariat. The lack of professional advancement opportunities for foreign workers is seen as a long-term sociopolitical problem.

Insurance Programs

Like all other employees, foreign workers are required to contribute to mandatory work-related insurance programs. When participation is optional, as in supplementary pension programs, foreign workers may subscribe if they so choose. In all three countries, foreign workers are covered by employment-related health, accident, disability/death, and social security insurance.

Aliens suffer proportionally far more work-related accidents, disabilities, and deaths than do native workers. In France, foreign workers comprise less than 10 percent of the total work force but account for 22.5 percent of work-related accidents.[13] One of four workers killed in France is foreign. In Germany, the foreign-worker accident rate is 25 percent higher than the indigenous rate.[14]

Most major labor-exporting countries have signed bilateral social security agreements that provide social security payments to retired foreign workers who return home. Some pension-fund payments are not to be made outside of the host society, particularly in Switzerland and France, but foreign workers with pension rights can request a lump sum payment before returning home. Foreign workers also have equal rights of access to company profit-sharing programs. In France, foreign workers who accept cash bonuses to return home forfeit their rights to social security.

Notes

1. W.R. Böhning, "International Migration in Western Europe: Reflections on the Past Five Years," *International Labour Review* 118 (1979):401-404.

2. See, for example, Gernot Müller-Serten, "Uncertainty a Cause of Anxiety, Meeting Told," *German Tribune,* November 9, 1980, p. 14.

3. Günter Matthes, "Bonn Works on a Set of Guidelines to Hasten Integration," *German Tribune,* March 23, 1980, p. 5.

4. George Minet, "Marginalité ou participation? Migrants et relations professionelles en europe occidentale," *Revue internationale du travail* 117 (1978):26-27.

5. Thomas Schaffroth, "Nationalistische Haltung Überwinden," *Berner Tagwacht,* March 30, 1977.

6. *DGB Report* 12 (1978):15.

7. Matthes, "Bonn Works on a Set of Guidelines," p. 5.

8. E. Hildebrandt and W. Olle, *Ihr Kampf ist unser Kampf. Ursachen, Verlauf and Perspektiven der Aüslanderstreiks 1973 in der BRD,* (Offenbach: Verlag 2000, 1975), pp. 79-87.

9. Betriebszelle Ford der Arbeiterkampf, *Streik bei Ford-Köln* (Cologne: Rosa Luxemburg Verlag, 1973).

10. *Revue syndicale suisse* (April 1975):101, 113, and Union syndicale suisse, *Rapport d'activité 1969-71* (Bern: Union Syndicale Suisse, 1972), p. 55.

11. Information kindly provided by Hannelore Koehler of the German Information Center.

12. *Le monde,* October 29, 1975, p. 32.

13. CGT-CFDT Press Conference, February 17, 1975, annex 3, p. 16.

14. *Problèmes économiques,* November 29, 1972, p. 16, and *L'unité,* February 27, 1976, p. 13.

Social Policies

The tension between the original policy assumption that foreign workers would be a temporary work force and the slow realization that foreign workers and their dependents have become part of the fabric of Western European society has largely shaped the evolution of social policies toward migrants. The Swiss dramatist Max Frisch once succinctly expressed this tension: the Europeans asked for workers, but men came.[1]

Initially foreign workers were not considered part of Western European society but with specific social problems and needs. However, by the early 1970s, as the permanency of foreign workers became evident and the severity of integration problems associated with it manifest, Western European states reinforced the social rights of migrant workers and sought to foster their integration (but not their assimilation) through social policy. Still, the social status of foreign workers and their dependents in Western Europe remains disfavored in contrast to that of the citizen population. This situation has given rise to considerable sociopolitical discord and apprehension on the part of Western Europeans.

Family Accommodation and Policies toward the Second Generation

Dependents, their schooling and vocational opportunities, housing, and sociopolitical rights are the focus of social policies toward migrant workers. Of these, the question of family entry and subsequent residency undoubtedly is the most important to migrant workers and has the most significant long-term implications for the host societies.

Over half of the total alien population of France and Germany is now comprised of dependents (table 7-1). Since the bans on further recruitment have become operative, the percentage of economically active to inactive foreigners has fallen considerably. France and Germany each contain populations of migrant children estimated at well over 800,000. Still, it is thought that only 64 percent of all foreign-worker dependents eligible to come to France have done so.[2] In Germany, it is estimated that an additional 1 million dependents might eventually choose to join foreigners employed there.[3] French and German family-support or allocation policies, which differentiate between dependents in Western Europe and those in

Table 7-1
Foreign-Worker Employment and Total Alien Populations, 1974-1980

Year	Foreigners Employed	Total Alien Population
France		
1974	1,900,000	4,038,000
1975	1,900,000	4,106,000
1976	1,584,000	4,205,000
1977	1,584,000	4,237,000
1978	1,643,000	4,170,000
1979		4,124,000
1980		4,148,000
Federal Republic of Germany		
1974	2,360,000	4,127,000
1975	2,171,000	4,089,000
1976	1,937,000	3,948,000
1977	1,889,000	3,948,000
1978	1,971,000	3,981,000
1979	2,067,000	4,144,000
1980	2,072,000[a]	4,453,000
Switzerland[b]		
1974	593,000	1,064,000
1975	553,000	1,012,000
1976	516,000	958,000
1977	492,000	932,000
1978	489,000	898,000
1979	491,000	884,000
1980	496,000	885,000

Sources: Système d'observation permanente des migrations, *1978 Report* (Paris Organization of Economic and Community Development, 1979); *Week in Germany,* November 26, 1980; *Le Monde,* June 26, 1981.
[a]As of June 1980.
[b]Not including frontier and seasonal workers.

the homeland, have encouraged family unification in those two countries. Under these policies, foreign-worker dependents receive payments that are adjusted to lower costs of living in the homelands and consequently pay less to dependents in the homelands than they do to dependents in Western Europe. Children of an Algerian worker in France, for example, would receive considerably less in monetary support if they are in Algeria than they would if they were in France. Family allocation payments are made to both citizen and resident noncitizen families and are financed primarily by employer taxes (or as the French unions contend, deferred wages) levied on the employment of both nationals and aliens.

Foreign populations in Western Europe also have been augmented by the births of migrant-worker children on alien soil. Thirty percent of all live births in Switzerland are the children of foreigners, while 16 and 10 percent of all live births in Germany and France, respectively, are of alien parentage.[4] Since 1970, 600,000 children have been born to foreigners in Germany, and it is estimated that in the decade 1980-1990 an additional 1 million foreign children will be born.[5] Children born of foreign workers in France can choose to become French citizens upon age eighteen. The naturalization possibilities of foreign-worker children born in Germany and Switzerland currently are slim, but both governments are considering easing their stringent naturalization requirements for foreign-worker children born on their soil. The increasing numbers of foreign workers who marry citizens now benefit from facilitated naturalization procedures.

The long-term significance of decisions in the domain of family entry generally was not appreciated until it was realized that the consequences of these policies were irreversible. Especially in Switzerland and Germany, which pointedly proclaimed that they were not immigration countries, public authorities originally made little provision for foreign-worker dependents. Foreign workers in Switzerland, for example, once had to wait for ten years before their dependents were allowed to join them. However, as the personal hardships of migrant workers occasioned by their family separation were publicized, barriers to family entry were removed. In France, family entry was facilitated as part of a long-term repopulation strategy. The French encouraged dependents of "assimilable" foreign-worker nationality groups (Spaniards and Portuguese) to join foreign workers by easing work restrictions on dependents and providing social assistance but did not ease restrictions on "unassimilable" nationality groups (North Africans). Today the French government does not encourage family entry from any labor-source country despite continuing calls from some Gaullists, such as Michel Debré, to do so.

In France and Germany, foreign workers must wait one year before they can petition officials to grant visas to their dependents, generally limited to the spouse and minor children under eighteen. In Switzerland, most migrant workers must wait for fifteen months before they can apply to bring in their families.[6] Seasonal permit holders in Switzerland and non-Spanish seasonal workers in France are not allowed to bring in their families. In all three countries, foreign workers must satisfy authorities that there is adequate housing for family members and that the worker is regularly employed and has the means to support the family before family visas are issued. Family members must pass medical examinations to be admitted. Dependents are not expected to seek work immediately upon reunification, though large numbers of dependents have sought and received work permits, thereby partially nullifying the impact of the 1973-1974 bans on the further recruitment of foreign workers.

Spouses and children reaching the age of eighteen generally are granted work permits within limitations dictated by priority to indigenous workers.

Government efforts to restrict the granting of work permits to dependents have collapsed in the face of migrant protests and fears of integration problems stemming from the unemployment of migrant children. In all three countries, the second generation of migrant children question is seen as a severe social problem because of their lack of educational and vocational skills. In the hopes of curbing juvenile delinquency of these foreigners and preventing the creation of a potentially disruptive mass of unemployed teenagers belonging to neither the homeland nor host societies, European states have granted work permits to migrant children despite their bans of foreign-worker recruitment. Migrant children now are allowed into apprenticeship and vocational training programs in order to enhance their employment opportunities. However, the language and other educational problems of second-generation migrant children result in most of them entering the job market as unskilled workers, like their fathers.

Migrant-Child Education

Swiss, French, and German law make school attendance by foreign-worker children compulsory. In France, over 550,000 foreign children are enrolled in public schools, compared to some 500,000 in Germany.[7] The overall percentage of foreign pupils in terms of school enrollment in France is 7.7 percent, while foreign pupils represent 6.2 percent of all students in German elementary schools.

The presence of foreign children in school systems is not uniform. In major German cities, 30 to 40 percent of all school beginners are foreign.[8] The concentration of foreign-worker children in certain schools has prompted Frankfurt authorities to take the exceptional step of busing pupils to promote equal educational opportunities.[9] In all three countries, special bilingual remedial education programs for migrant children have been instituted.

European schools increasingly provide for parallel education in the native tongues of foreign-worker children. Homeland governments also play a role in migrant-children education by sponsoring extracurricular courses taught in the native language of the children. Despite genuine efforts on the part of European educators to respond to the special problems encountered by these children, the children of migrant workers generally do not fare well in school.[10] In Germany, only one-third of them attending finish grade school.[11] Of those who go on to high school, fewer than half graduate, compared to 80 percent of German students.[12] Much of the same is true in France and Switzerland. Most foreign-worker children end up in trade schools where they have difficulty completing courses. Torn between two languages and cultures, many foreign-worker children master neither the language of their country of residence nor that of their parents.

Migrant-Adult Education

Since many foreign workers are illiterate and their children brought up in Western Europe often end up as illiterate young adults, the advanced industrial societies of Western Europen paradoxically contain large populations of illiterates. In France, it is estimated that there are 1 million illiterates among the 4 million migrants.[13] The illiteracy problem along with a perception that adult migrant educational deficiencies will adversely affect their children have combined to prompt European governments to establish adult education programs. Governments subsidize private and semigovernmental migrant educational associations, which teach foreign workers and their dependents the language of the host society. Foreign workers' wives and young adults also have some access to special professional and general educational programs designed for them and staffed by specially trained teachers. Most adult education programs for migrants are recent so it is difficult to evaluate their effect.

Housing

After family entry, housing is the most salient concern for foreign workers. France, Switzerland, and Germany make initial work contracts contingent upon access to adequate housing. Housing regulations specify minimal spatial living areas per migrant and require normal access to utilities and cleanliness. These regulations are difficult to enforce, though, and violations are rampant.

Migrants are frequently placed in company housing upon arrival. In Germany, 34 percent of all foreigners live in company-supplied housing while 65 percent live in private housing.[14] The spartan quality of life in company housing, the lack of privacy, and frequently the physical remoteness of the housing from social centers have tended to increase the social isolation of migrant workers.

Many of these same problems also occur when foreign workers find housing on the open market. There is a housing shortage in Europe, and foreign workers, because of their lower salaries, unfamiliarity with local housing markets, and discrimination, are at a competitive disadvantage. Hence they tend to concentrate in rundown urban centers where they often subdivide housing units to lower rents and increase savings. In Germany, it is estimated that 25 percent of the foreign population are housed four to a room.[15] Over the last decade, foreign-worker ghettoes have developed in most major European cities. These quarters tend to become homeland microcosms where native languages are spoken and homeland cultural matrices recreated.

Perhaps the most extreme manifestations of the foreign-worker ghetto phenomenon were the *bidonvilles*, which dotted the urban landscape throughout France in the 1960s. *Bidonvilles* resembled the Hoovervilles of the Great Depression in the United States and generally consisted of makeshift shacks without running water, electricity, or proper sanitation. Living conditions in these areas were so deplorable that the government systematically razed them and relocated many of the displaced foreigners in government-built housing in the early 1970s. The French semigovernmental authority charged with the construction and administering of housing for foreign workers now has some 77,000 residents. However, some 10,000 to 20,000 residents refused to pay their rents to protest living conditions and what they regarded as unwarranted rent increases for over three years. This strike cost the French government about $50 million in lost rents and considerable public embarassment as the strikers focused attention upon the deficiencies of migrant housing and the government resorted to harsh measures to end the strike, including deportation of seventeen strike leaders, but nonetheless did not succeed in crushing the strike.

The substandard nature of much migrant housing has given rise to protests and demonstrations throughout Western Europe. Especially when migrant families or several roommates are killed by fires or gas leaks, public indignation over migrant housing conditions prompts governments to announce ameliorative measures.[17] While foreigners increasingly have access to public housing and the French government provides subsidies to city governments that undertake to renovate foreign-worker slums, actual remedial measures by European public authorities generally have lagged behind what has been promised.

Budgetary Support

A major reason for lagging vocational training or housing programs on behalf of foreigners is inadequate funding; however, European governments have significantly increased their budgetary support for social programs on behalf of foreigners in recent years. The French budget for social services to migrants and their dependents in 1975 (four francs per dollar) broke down as follows (in millions of dollars):

1. General governmental appropriations: $132.9.
2. Social action funds: $61.4.
3. Family support allowance: $6.0 (1974).
4. ONI: $0.7 (1974).
5. Employer contributions: $125.0 (estimated).
6. Other: $125.0 (estimated)[18]

Items 2, 3, and 5 represent spending of revenue mainly obtained from employer taxes. These types of expenditures apparently are not included in the following breakdown of German spending in 1976.[19] (The German figures were arrived at by calculating 1.75 DM to equal one dollar and are given in millions of dollars.)

1. Social welfare services: $9.14.
2. Counseling centers: $1.14.
3. German language courses: $0.85.
4. Vocational training: $0.40.
5. Foreign youth employment training: $0.29.
6. Overall social integration: $17.14.

Public spending for foreign workers is justified on the grounds that the foreigners are taxed as citizens are and hence have a right to governmental services. It is widely believed, though, that foreign workers use regular social services more so than citizens do. Conclusive evidence of disproportionate migrant usage of social services is rare, however. Two recent French governmental reports reached contradictory conclusions concerning the social costs of foreign workers because of the complex methodological problems of ascertaining aggregate service utilization.[20] The report contending that the social cost of migrants was high found that: foreign workers have higher family allowance and dependent-care costs for the government than do French workers; for every 100 contributors to social security, 120 foreigners as compared to 90 Frenchmen are covered by social security protection; health and sickness payments to foreigners average 50 percent more than payments to Frenchmen; and migrant use of maternity wards and hospitals is disproportionate given high migrant birth and accident rates.[21]

Critics of this report were quick to note that migrant populations are young, thereby reducing health care costs for the aged, and that medical examinations during recruitment screen out many unhealthy applicants. Further, they objected that the conclusions did not take into account the fact that many social services for migrants in France are financed by money saved because of family-allowance-payment differentials for migrant children in France and those abroad.

While public debates in all three countries over foreign-worker usage of social services continue in part because of inconclusive evidence, it is highly probable that the perception of migrants' overburdening social services contributed to recruitment bans. The widespread belief that migrants abuse or swamp social services has fueled xenophobic reactions. The potential for xenophobic reactions in this domain increases as economic difficulties lead to calls for cutbacks in social welfare spending.

This socioeconomic dilemma is illustrated by recent events in Germany. The neonazi National Democratic Party of Germany (NPD) made "Foreigners out. Germany is for Germans" its campaign slogan during the October 1980 election. Although the NPD touched a sympathetic cord among German voters, it failed to gain votes for its extreme proposal.

The victorious Social Democratic party of Chancellor Helmut Schmidt made the integration of foreigners the top domestic priority for 1981. However, integration could not result in additional public outlays because of a projected 1981 budget deficit of $17 billion, 2.8 percent of GNP. The Free Democrats, junior partners in the government, are pressing to reduce outlays by loosening the social security safety net. Hence, budgetary limitations preclude expansive new efforts on behalf of foreigners.

Associational and Political Rights

European social policies toward migrants also pertain to migrant associational and political rights. In the effort to reduce integration problems, governments progressively have reinforced the potential for migrant participation in public affairs. Foreign workers are not powerless and voiceless as is so frequently charged (appendix J). This characterization has tended to obfuscate the considerable nonelectoral civic rights and political resources of European guest workers.

The political status of foreign workers is one of the most controversial aspects of Western European foreign-worker policies. As noncitizens, foreigners are not permitted to vote in Western European national legislative or executive elections. But in light of the numerical importance of foreign populations in many European states, their electoral disenfranchisement is a factor of considerable significance. Labor-oriented parties feel especially disadvantaged because they assume foreign workers would vote for them.

Workers and the Homeland Government

Foreign workers are workers at home abroad. Despite emigrating, they remain citizens and participants in their native political systems. An important dimension of their political status involves the degree of host-country toleration of homeland-oriented political activities ranging from voting to protests. Depending on the electoral laws of the various homelands, foreign workers may be allowed to vote abroad if the host government consents. France and Germany, for example, allow Spanish and Portuguese workers to vote at consulates, while Switzerland refuses this right to foreigners. Some homelands, most notably Turkey, require emigrants to return home to vote. In the case of Italian workers in Germany, transportation home for electoral purposes is subsidized.

Generally European governments tolerate homeland-oriented political activities among foreign workers up to the point of political violence. In several cases, domestic political violence has spilled over to migrant-worker communities in Western Europe. Despite their restriction status, foreign workers often enjoy more freedom of political expression in Western Europe than in their native lands. This has contributed to the development of political opposition in the ranks of some foreign-worker groups that has complicated diplomatic relations.

Homeland governments usually sponsor organizations intended to maintain emigrant contacts with the homeland and, frequently, to prevent the alienation of sympathy from the homeland government. The 60,000-member strong Amicale des algériens en europe (AAE), for example, is virtually the overseas branch of the ruling Algerian political party, the Front de Libération Nationale. Extensive consular networks have developed, and local consulates often sponsor cultural associations with political overtones. Among the Portuguese in France, for example, there are some four hundred associations mainly linked to consulates, the Catholic church, and also to opposition parties.[22] Among Turks in Germany, there are some 112 associations, often bitterly divided along political lines. The German Ministry of the Interior has estimated that 10 percent of all Turks living in Germany belong to politically oriented associations.[23]

Participation in Host-Society Public Life

Foreign workers generally enjoy liberties of expression, including press and assembly, and largely are free to form their own associations or to join indigenous ones. France is somewhat more restrictive than its eastern neighbors in this area because of the stipulation that aliens in France observe political neutrality. In Germany and Switzerland, foreign workers enjoy the right to join political parties, while foreign-party membership is tolerated in France. Ironically, France apparently boasts the party with the largest foreign-worker membership; the French Communist Party (PCF) includes 25,000 foreign members.[24] The most important restrictions on migrant political activity stem from the stipulation that the public order not be endangered. Political violence by migrants is not tolerated.

In recent years, foreign workers have played a prominent part in protest movements on issues ranging from racism and discrimination against foreigners to factory closings or housing conditions. Their protest marches are particuarly significant in France where the opposition parties have supported foreign workers against the government in cases like the SONACOTRA rent strike which pitted up to 20,000 foreigners dissatisfied with rent increases and living conditions in government-run dormitories against the government from late 1975 to 1980. Foreign workers in Switzerland and Germany have been less active than in France, in part due to the absence of violent racism. Murders of North African workers in France, such as resulted from a bombing of the Algerian consulate in Marseille in 1973, periodically spark massive protest demonstrations and strikes by foreign workers.

Foreign workers can communicate their specific problems or desires to public authorities through special advisory boards and councils. These are consultative councils only, however, and even though elections may be held to select foreign-worker representatives, they have no genuine decision-making power. Germany and Switzerland have extensive networks of coordination councils and contact centers from the local level of government through to the national which intend to facilitate foreign-worker representation in public policymaking. France's system of local councils is less extensive but growing. Foreign-worker representatives often are selected by trade unions, religious organizations, or foreign associations. While foreign workers generally are dissatisfied with their voice in European governments, these consultative organs have improved foreign worker-governmental communication and have promoted an awareness of migrant problems. Some critics have charged, though, that consultative councils offer only the illusion of participation and, hence, serve to pacify foreign workers rather than genuinely help them.

European socialist parties generally endorse the idea of foreign-worker electoral participation in local elections, such as already occurs in Sweden. However, even within socialist parties, there is resistance to granting aliens voting rights, and constitutions currently bar aliens from municipal voting. Political controversy over migrant voting nights has been most intense in France where the Socialist Party has promised to press for migrant local-voting rights if it comes into power, while the French Communist Party strongly opposes the grant of such rights to foreign workers.

Notes

1. Frisch's now well-known aphorism is, "Man hat Arbeitskraefte gerufen, und es kommen Menschen." Cited by Klaus Lefringhausen, "Wirtschaftesethische Aspekte fuer lokale Aktionen," in Rene Leudesdorff and Horst Zillessen, eds., *Gastarbeiter-Mitbuerger* (Gelnhausen: Burckhardthaus, 1971), p. 192.

2. "Statistiques Annotées," *Perspectives,* January 27, 1977.

3. *Social Report* (German Government Publication), October 1976 and February 1978.

4. *Sozialpolitische Umschau,* no. 14 (1978).

5. *Social Report,* February, 1978.

6. *Problèmes humains des travailleurs étrangers et leurs familles* (Bern: Commission fédérale consultative pour le problème des étrangers, 1976), p. 14.

7. Lutz Drebsbach, "Timb Bomb Warning over Foreign Children," *German Tribune,* September 2, 1979, p. 4, and *Le dossier de l'immigration* (November 1978): Entry 6.

8. *Der Arbeitgeber,* September 23, 1977, and *Die Welt,* February 8, 1978.

9. Jutta Roitsch, "School Bussing Project Aims at Quickening Integration," *German Tribune,* June 29, 1980, p. 12.

10. "Report Demands Equal Opportunities for Foreign Children," *German Tribune,* April 8, 1979.

11. *German Tribune,* October 28, 1979, p. 12.

12. G. Matthes, "Bonn Works on a Set of Guidelines to Hasten Integration," *German Tribune,* March 23, 1980, p. 5.

13. *Le monde,* December 4, 1974.

14. *Statistiches Jahrbuch* (February 1974): figure 253-380.

15. Rudolph Blitz, "A Benefit-Cost Analysis of Foreign Workers in West Germany, 1957-1973," *Kyklos* 30 (1977):501.

16. Secrétaire d'état a la condition des travailleurs immigrés, press communiqué, April 24, 1979.

17. See, for example, *Le monde,* May 11, 1973.

18. Ibid., February, 15, 1979.

19. Sozialpolitische Umschau, July 1976.

20. *Le monde,* February 15, July 5, 1977.

21. "Statistiques Annotées," *Perspectives,* January 27, 1977.

22. *Le monde,* April 24, 1976, p. 4.

23. Matthes, "Bon Works on a Set of Guidelines," p. 5.

24. *Le monde,* April 29-30, 1979, and *L'humanité,* April 28, 1979.

The European Dilemma: Integration or Return

With the limited exception of France, which encouraged the immigration of "assimilable" foreign workers until the mid-1970s, European governments did not expect foreign-worker employment to result in large-scale permanent immigration. Foreign workers were expected to be a temporary or complementary work force, which eventually returned home. To the contrary, a large number of foreign workers have become long-term residents of Europe, and foreign-worker policies have become de facto but still not fully acknowledged immigration policies. Therein lies the crux of the European dilemma. Long-term foreign-worker residency or immigration is considered undesirable because of the integration problems associated with foreign workers, especially during a period of economic recession. Yet repatriation of foreign workers and their dependents who do not voluntarily return has proven to be a difficult, if not impossible, goal to attain.

Shortcomings of the Assumption of Rotation and Return Policy

In retrospect, one fundamental miscalculation of European alien-labor policies was underestimation of the human dimensions of alien-worker employment. As foreign-worker policies were progressively improved over the years, facilitating family entry and other measures to improve the lot of foreign workers, European governments undercut their own policy goal of short-term foreign-worker employment. This goal, ironically, was further undermined by postwar Europe's sustained economic growth. Originally it had been assumed that foreign workers would return home during periods of recession. However, with the limited exception of 1967, such a recession did not occur until 1973. By the time unfavorable economic conditions moved governments to implement the expectation of return, many foreign workers had such long continuous residency due to permit renewal that they could not be forced to return home.

Denial of work and residency permit renewal is the administrative essence of a forcible return policy. It was widely assumed, however, that foreign workers would not want to remain for long periods of time in Western Europe. Hence, it was felt that migrant-worker repatriation would occur naturally after foreign workers amassed savings and then voluntarily returned home. This expectation of voluntary migrant-worker return was bolstered by sociological surveys finding that most foreign workers expected to remain in the host societies for only several years and by labor-source country policies calling for the eventual reintegration of emigrant workers. Consequently European governments, especially the Swiss and Germans, expected the sojourns of individual foreign workers to be short term, and they did not exercise the administrative prerogative of nonrenewal of permits in any systematic way.

The complacency regarding foreign-worker repatriation resulted in part from what European scholars now call the foreign workers' "illusion of return."[1] The foreigners' expectation of a relatively brief sojourn in Western Europe frequently was not realized in practice. Foreign-worker return rates fluctuated by nationality. However, even the small percentage who did not return translated into large population additions because of the enormous and unexpected volume of postwar migrations.[2]

Even after foreign workers had become long-term residents of the host societies, with little possibility of one day returning home, they often persisted in believing that they shortly would repatriate. This pattern of illusion is partially explained as a psychological response to perceived discrimination. However, migrant workers also came to find return increasingly difficult because of the lack of suitable employment for them at home and the necessity of readjustment to traditional society, an adjustment especially difficult for their children.

Even after the illusion-of-return phenomenon had been discerned, though, European governments persisted in regarding return as something that was desired by most migrants. This continuing misperception concerning the personal plans of a sizable fraction of foreign workers was underscored by the German government's recent reaffirmation that foreign workers wanted to return home while a survey of foreign-worker households released almost simultaneously found that half of the foreigners intended to stay permanently.[3]

Despite official policies encouraging migrant reintegration into homelands, labor-exporting countries did little to facilitate the return of their emigrants. In all likelihood, homeland governmental public commitments to migrant-worker returns have been largely rhetorical, designed to assuage nationalistic feelings and to justify governmental cooperation in migrant-worker recruitment. Governments can facilitate return of emigrant workers by providing housing for migrants and their families, training opportunities, special social services and tax or customs incentives. But all such measures are costly for countries already burdened with high unemployment, housing shortages and struggling economies. Certainly repatriation goals such as the Algerian return policy have reinforced the perception of temporary foreign-worker sojourns. Yet despite the recent

Franco-Algerian accords, it cannot be said that Algeria has aggressively pursued migrant reintegration. Although it does more to facilitate the return of emigrants than virtually any other labor-exporting country, it resists forcible repatriation of its citizens.[4] Further, like other labor-exporting countries, Algeria continues to face unemployment problems and still depends on migrant-worker cash remittances to provide food and other basic amenities for a significant portion of its population, especially in rural areas. Hence, there is reason to believe that migrant return is more of a slogan than policy except, perhaps, concerning skilled migrant workers.

The combination of misplaced confidence in migrant plans to return, homeland reluctance or inability to reintegrate emigrants, and the prolonged economic expansion caused European governments to neglect the final link in the temporary-worker policy chain: return. During the 1960s and early 1970s, foreign-worker permits were routinely renewed. European governments probably could have replaced foreign workers having two or three years of residency with fresh recruits, but three factors mitigated against this. First, employers had to pay recruitment fees for the introduction of new foreign workers. Experienced foreign workers were already in place, and these workers had priority over potential recruits still waiting in the homelands. Second, the replacement of foreign workers could be costly in terms of training and adaptation time, although foreign workers characteristically worked in jobs requiring little training. Third, integration policies favoring foreign workers were implausible for short-term international migrants. Family entry rights, trade-union affiliation, and language-training courses, for example, would have little utility if foreign workers were required to return after two or three years of residency. These considerations, plus multinational and bilateral diplomatic instruments that enjoin the granting of permanent residency rights after set periods of residence, undermined the goal of return. In the one clear-cut case prior to the 1973-1974 bans on non-EEC foreign-worker recruitment where systematic nonrenewal of work and residency permits was envisaged, Bavarian state authorities were rebuffed in their effort to deny permit renewals by the German government. Bavarian policy objectives were deemed inhumane, contrary to German treaty commitments, and inimical to integration policies. Western European governments did not actually have a viable administrative option of forcing out a large number of migrants when worsening economic conditions increased pressures for repatriation. Such a policy, which might be termed the myth of rotation policy, when applied to foreign workers employed in permanent jobs would have been incompatible with democratic, humanitarian principles.

The number of foreign workers who had qualified for permanent or nonrevocable work and residency permits by 1976 bears testimony to the administrative impossibility of forcing out massive numbers of foreign workers through denial of permit renewal. In Germany, it was estimated that 1.2 million guest workers had permanent residency status or could obtain it either as EEC nationals or because of the length of their residency on German soil.[5] Over 800,000 alien workers had lived in Germany for ten years or longer, and fully 56.7 percent of German foreign workers had been there over seven years.[6] In Switzerland, where five years of continuous residency also qualified foreign workers for nonrevocable status, 79 percent of all foreign workers had lived there for seven years or longer.[7] By 1976, over two-thirds of Swiss foreign workers had privileged status. Similarly, in France, most foreign workers could not be sent home against their will. France has adopted a policy of nonforcible return, although it uses return bonuses to encourage voluntary repatriation.

Return Incentives

In all three countries, nonforcible or freely willed foreign-worker repatriation is regarded as desirable. To this end, special programs designed to facilitate migrant return have been inaugurated, ranging from outright cash payments to foreigners who renounce their residency rights to foreign aid earmarked to create jobs for returning workers in the homelands. Most of these incentive-to-return programs have been in existence for only a few years, so they are difficult to evaluate. However, early indications are that it is much easier to recruit foreign workers than to get them to return.

Certainly the most controversial program of this sort is the French policy of giving foreign workers and their dependents cash payments to return home. The idea first was proposed in Germany, but the German government rejected it as incongruent with nonforcible return policy.[8] The notion was also rejected by the French government at first. But deteriorating economic conditions, especially soaring unemployment, caused the French to reconsider. The French cash-payment program initially applied to only unemployed foreign workers. By 1977, though, eligibility for the cash payments was extended to all foreign workers with five years of residency and their dependents.[9] Today an eligible foreign worker who renounces residency and working rights in France is entitled to receive a cash payment of 10,000 FF (roughly $2,000). Dependents of foreign workers receive lesser payments (up to 5,000 FF) if they return with the head of household. The government also pays transportation costs for any returning foreigners. Returning aliens receive the money only after they have left French territory.

Between June 1977 and December 1978, 23,300 applicants out of a total of 24,461 requests were accepted as qualifying for the cash payments. Including dependents, about 45,000 foreigners—the government had hoped

for 100,000—have returned home under the program.[10] This figure
represents only 3 to 4 percent of the total number of foreign employees eligible under the program. Roughly half of all foreign workers who
repatriated during this period took advantage of the return bonus. It is
thought that many of the returnees were near retirement age, and it was
primarily European foreign workers, considered less difficult to integrate,
who participated in the program. Portuguese and Spaniards represented 42
and 30 percent, respectively, of those returning with cash bonuses; North
Africans represented only 16 percent. Hence, from the French government's
perspective, the least assimilable foreigners were also the least likely to
apply for the cash bonuses. The governmment's announcement in 1980 of a
special four-month salary return incentive to Algerians, which the government maintained would foster 35,000 returns per year (in conjunction with
a training program option) starting in 1983, was greeted with skepticism.

The *aide au retour* program's mixed success is attributable in part to
widespread political opposition to it. French trade unions have been particularly vociferous in denouncing it as prejudicial to foreign workers, as
have church and foreign-worker assistance groups.[11] The Conseil d'état, a
judicial council overseeing the constitutionality of French administrative
procedures, declared the program to be unconstitutional.[12] However, the
French government continued the program in contravention of the Conseil
d'état ruling.[13]

Opposition to the program centers mainly on the belief that foreign
workers forfeit much of their tax contributions in accepting the return
bonus. The French government maintains that the bonus reflects the
average sum of governmental payments that would be made to unemployed
foreign workers if they remained. Further, it is pointed out that the program is voluntary. According to opponents of the program, however, the
aide au retour is a transparent attempt by the government to rid France of
foreign workers who were welcomed in a period of economic expansion,
who contributed much to French prosperity, and who now are being enticed
to return against their best interests. Opponents of the program also charge
that foreign returnees are made to pay the cost of the recession in an ineq-
uitable fashion.

The question of organizing foreign-worker repatriation has raised
political passions everywhere, but programs in other countries aimed at
facilitating migrant return have been less controversial, in part because they
too have been largely ineffective. Germany has relied mainly on joint projects with homeland countries to encourage repatriation. Most notably, Germany has signed bilateral agreements with Greece and Turkey committing
the signatories to co-finance the creation of jobs of returning migrants. The
German-Turkish agreement stipulates that both governments should provide 6 million *DM* apiece (roughly $2.8 million) for job creation.[14] The

German and Turkish governments also cooperate in encouraging Turkish workers to invest their savings in joint capital ventures creating jobs in Turkey. Between 50,000 and 100,000 Turkish workers in Germany have bought shares in these companies. As of 1977, the 128 joint-venture companies had created twenty-eight firms in Turkey employing some 2,500 workers. Another one hundred or so additional firms were in various stages of planning. The total capital of these companies amounted to $375 million.[15] Despite the considerable publicity given foreign-worker investment plans, such as the Turkish joint capital ventures, they have had only minimal impact so far on overall unemployment in the homelands, and they have created only a few jobs for returning migrants.

Opening up more vocational training opportunities to foreign workers prior to their return home has been advocated as a key component in an organized, equitable repatriation program. While all three governments have accepted the principle of enhanced vocational training for returnees, they have been slow in developing programs that give foreign workers marketable skills upon return. Foreign-worker access to vocational training, though, has improved, and as a result of recent Franco-Algerian negotiations, it seems that a model program training Algerians before their return might soon begin. A few thousand migrants in Germany currently are trained as apprentices for several years before returning to their homelands. European incentive-to-return programs have been supplemented by governmental efforts to distribute information necessary to migrants for their return.

Integration

Barring radical and highly improbable changes such as the adoption of forcible return policies, the reluctance of millions of foreign workers and their dependents to return home leaves European governments with no choice but to facilitate the integration of these foreigners—even if integration efforts make eventual repatriation less likely. The alternative to integration is perceived to be the development of sociopolitically disruptive minority classes. Indeed, some believe that European integration efforts might already be too late to prevent the development of serious long-term social problems.

In all three countries, the effort to integrate foreign workers has necessitated extensive coordination of administrative services. In keeping with European social partnership traditions of formal governmental consultation of key interest groups in policy matters, trade unions, religious and civil-rights organizations, employer representatives, and foreign-worker interest groups have been associated with local and national governmental officials in recommending policies. Major policies concerning foreign workers usually result from consultations through these structures, although the French tradition of highly centralized government and deep political cleavages has rendered its advisory councils on foreign-worker matters much less effective. Even in Germany, though, a recent series of reforms proposed by a federal-level commission (the Kuehn Report) seem unlikely to be adopted in the foreseeable future.

The Europeans have found that integration policy affects all aspects of their societies—from education to labor-management relations. Hence, the overall administration of foreign-worker policies has become more complex through the years in contrast to the relatively simple task of administering foreign workers when it was assumed they would be a temporary supplement to the work force. After long ignoring the complex problems stemming from foreign-worker policies, comprehensive coordination structures now testify to European recognition of the sociopolitical consequences of nonimmigrant labor policy. This hidden dimension of foreign-worker policy involves potential long-term problems, which the Europeans only belatedly are trying to remedy through integration policies.

The integration program adopted by all three governments in the 1970s included provisions for better housing, family reunification, more vocational and language training, enhanced opportunities for migrant interest articulation at the local and national governmental levels, special educational aids and counseling for dependents, partial elimination of employment and residency restrictions, and improved information services (including radio and television programs). In addition, governments adopted public relations measures designed to promote foreign-native harmony and to increase public awareness of problems encountered by migrants. Whether these integration measures will prevent the development of long-term minority problems is not yet clear.

Notes

1. This term appears to have been coined by Rudolf Braun in his *Soziokulturelle Probleme der Eingliederung italienischer Arbeitskraefte in der Schweiz* (Erlenback-Zurich: Reutsch, 1970), pp. 473, 488. Also see H. le Masne, "Le retour des algériens au pays," *Economie et humanisme* 221 (1975):9-10.

2. W.R. Bohning, "Guestworker Employment, with Special Reference to the Federal Republic of Germany, France and Switzerland—Lessons for the United States" (College Park: University of Maryland, Center for Philosophy and Public Policy paper, 1980).

3. Christian Schneider, "Official Attitude Outdated as People Don't Return Home," *German Tribune*, September 2, 1979, p. 4.

4. On Algerian measures facilitating emigrant return, see a paper by Stephen Adler, "The Organization of Return Migration: A Preliminary Analysis of the Recent Experience of France and Algeria" (Paris: OECD, 1976).

5. *Christian Science Monitor*, November 1, 1976.

6. *Frankfurter Rundschau*, April 2, 1977.

7. "Evolution et effectif de la population étrangére resident en Suisse in 1976," *La vie economique* (April 1977): table 5.

8. *German Tribune*, March 7, 1974.

9. *Le monde*, June 18, 20, September 3, 29, 1977.

10. *Migrants nouvelles* (September 1979):5.

11. *Le monde*, October 18, 1977.

12. Ibid., November 27, 1978.

13. Information kindly provided by André Lebon, June 1979.

14. *Migrants nouvelles* (September 1979):28.

15. Winfried Didzoleit, "In der Fremde am Fliessband und in der Heimat Aktionar," *Frankfurter Rundschau*, Easter, 1977, p. 8.

9 Effects on Labor-Sending Societies

Assumptions concerning the beneficial impacts of foreign-labor programs upon Western European societies now are seen as less and less sound as sociopolitical problems mount and memories of the important economic contributions of migrant workers fade. A similar rethinking of the presumed positive effects of labor migration policies has taken place in emigrant-sending societies, where certain hidden costs of emigration policies have become apparent—especially the unmeasurable social dislocation caused by emigration.

Not all emigrant-sending societies entered into bilateral labor programs with unbridled confidence in the beneficial effects of such programs. In Algeria, the wisdom of allowing workers to emigrate to France in the immediate postrevolutionary period was hotly debated. However, those political elites favoring labor emigration prevailed because of huge unemployment problems, the prospect of increased cash-remittance flows, and the need for skilled workers. Officially at least, Algerian labor emigration policy was presumed to be temporary because the conditions necessitating it—unemployment, poverty, and a dearth of skilled personnel—would be abolished by an ambitious developmental strategy.

Labor migration was one component of an overall developmental strategy in the Algerian case. In most other emigrant-sending societies, the linkage between labor emigration and development plans was less articulated. It was assumed that labor emigration would benefit the sending societies mainly by reducing unemployment and generating remittance income. There is little, if any, evidence that emigrant-sending governments in the Mediterranean basin sought to shore themselves up politically by using labor emigration as a political safety valve to relieve potentially destabilizing unemployment.

The effects of emigrant labor programs upon sending societies can be broken down into three major areas: economic, social, and political. Evaluations of migrant labor influences upon sending countries usually stress economic effects over social and political ones, in part because of the difficulty of finding suitable indicators to measure effects in the last two categories. Nonetheless, the social and political consequences of labor emigration may be as important as the economic consequences.

Economic Consequences

Western European governments now have statistics on the outflow of foreign-worker remittances to the various sending countries. These remittance statistics do not represent the totality of wealth transfers between labor-host and -sending societies as a result of foreign-labor employment because foreign workers may keep savings in Western European banks, the transfer of nonmonetary wealth, such as cars bought in Western Europe and then sold in the homeland over vacation, is not included and some money transfers are not recorded, such as the money a foreign worker takes home on vacation. Foreign workers in Germany and Switzerland have no restraints on home remittances. In France, foreign workers are limited to sending home amounts of money equal to the pay they have received within three months of receiving that salary. Either the worker's employer or a financial intermediary must annotate the money transfers.

According to the ILO, the labor-sending countries of the Mediterranean basin together received some $7 billion in remittances from their some 7.5 million workers employed throughout Western Europe in 1974.[1] Table 9-1 presents the total remittances received from workers abroad by the six major emigrant-labor-sending countries of the OECD for the period 1974-1976. The significant declines in remittances received by Turkey and Portugal from emigrant workers after the recruitment halts are obvious. These declines seriously aggravated Portuguese and Turkish economies, already weakened by oil price increases and global recession. At first, it was thought the massive family reunification in the early 1970s had caused migrant remittances to decline, but recent French research has suggested that this factor, if anything, tends to increase remittance payments because a spouse or a child might enter the work force and thereby increase the aggregate income from which remittances are sent.[2] Overall economic conditions, of-

Table 9-1
Aggregate Receipt of Remittances, 1974-1976
(millions of dollars)

	1974	1975	1976
Turkey	1,425	1,300	983
Greece	645	734	803
Yugoslavia	1,621	1,695	1,878
Italy	753	979	1,370[a]
Spain	1,071	968	853
Portugal	1,100	539	683

Source: André Lebon, "Les transfers de fonds des travailleurs étrangers," in *Les travailleurs étrangers et le droit international,* ed. Société Française pour le Droit International (Paris: Editions A. Pedone, 1979), p. 370. Reprinted with permission.

ficial exchange rate imbalances, fear of devaluation, and political instability seem to account for the decline of remittances to Turkey and Portugal.

Table 9-2 suggests the economic importance of foreign-worker remittances to the same six OECD countries by comparing their remittance income and the total value of their product exports for 1973. Clearly remittances play a major role in the ability of labor-exporting countries to import industrial and consumer goods.

In table 9-3, the best statistical approximation of aggregate remittance outflows from France, Switzerland, and Germany to major labor-sending countries is presented. The Swiss statistics are unofficial and represent only the money transfers of nonprivileged-status foreign workers there. Hence only remittances from frontier, seasonal, and annual workers are included. The size of foreign-worker remittance outflows is an issue of some political sensitivity in all three countries because antiforeign-worker elements charge that remittance outflows sap job-creating investment. However, a not inconsiderable portion of remittances seems to be spent on imported goods from the host societies and, more importantly, the value of remittance outflows accruing to a labor-exporting country in a given year is small in comparison to the value of the aggregate expenditures it would have cost to raise natives to do the jobs done by foreigners. Labor-sending societies pay the costs of raising and educating foreign workers without any compensation from the host societies. Recently, though, proposals have been made to compensate the source societies directly in addition to indirect compensation through remittances.[3]

The remittance-sending proclivities of foreign workers vary by nationality groups as suggested by comparison in table 9-4 of their respective shares of the total alien work force and total remittance outflow in 1977 in Germany. The proclivities of various nationality groups to send remittances

Table 9-2
Remittance Inflows and Products Exported, 1973
(millions of dollars)

	Remittances	Products Exported	Remittances as a Percent of Products Exported
Turkey	1,183	1,318	90
Greece	735	1,454	51
Yugoslavia	1,398	3,025	46
Spain	1,185	5,178	23
Portugal	1,025	1,750	59

Source: André Lebon, "Les transfers de fonds des travailleurs étrangers," in *Les travailleurs étrangers et le droit international*, ed. Société Française pour le Droit International (Paris: Editions A. Pedone, 1979), p. 370. Reprinted with permission.

Table 9-3
Remittance Outflows from Switzerland, Germany, and France 1974-1976
(millions of dollars)

	Switzerland	Germany	France
1974	2,234	4,771	2,079
1975	2,097	3,771	2,061
1976	1,709	3,657	2,264

Source: Adapted from A. Lebon, "Les transfers de fonds des travailleurs étrangers," in *Les travailleurs étrangers et le droit international,* ed. Société Française pour le Droit International (Paris: Editions A. Pedone, 1979), pp. 371-374.

Note: Conversion rates: 4 FF = $1 1.75 SF = $1, and 1.75 DM = $1.

are influenced by such contextual factors as the exchange rate and, according to recent French research, by patterns pertaining to length of stay. Foreign workers with three to twelve years of residency send more money home than do shorter- or longer-term migrants.[4] In Germany in 1977 an average of $1,888 per foreign worker was sent home in the form of remittances.

The money that emigrants send home is obviously beneficial to their dependents who have remained there. They use it to pay for food, services, and consumer items that otherwise they might not have been able to afford. In some emigrant-worker-sending societies, remittances are a major source of income for entire regions. In Algeria, for example, the remittances have enabled the government to invest more funds in development projects because public funds did not have to be diverted to the consumption needs of predominantly agricultural areas.[5] Nevertheless often this money sent home is spent in ways that do not contribute to overall economic development.

The growing literature on the effects of emigrant labor programs upon labor-sending societies reveals that remittances often are spent upon imported consumer items and generally are not put into investments that respond to the developmental needs of emigrant-sending economies. In addition to providing for the basic needs of dependents, often including extended families in traditional societies, emigrant remittances characteristically are spent on improving lodgings or building new homes and buying televisions, radios, and other consumer goods that, according to some critics, amount to conspicuous consumption in terms of the personal amenities characteristic of developing societies. The image invoked by this literature is one of rural villages in Anatolia or the Porto-region of Portugal sprouting television antennas from the roofs of humble peasant lodgings to which a recent addition has been made. Another recurrent image is one of villages full of taxis that seldom are used or of tractors that are prestige items but of little practical use. Remittances thus tend to exacerbate demand-side infla-

Table 9-4
Total Alien Work Force in Germany and Total Remittance Outflow, by Nationality, 1977

	Alien Workers (in 1000s)	Percentage	Total Remittances (in U.S. Millions)	Percentage	Average Sum Remitted per Worker	Difference between Columns 2 and 4
Turkey	528	27.2	1,229	33.6	$2,328	+ 6.4%
Greece	179	9.2	371	10.2	2,073	+ 1.0
Yugoslavia	390	20.1	1,057	28.9	2,710	+ 8.8
Spain	111	5.1	257	7.0	2,315	− 1.3
Italy	276	14.3	457	12.5	1,656	− 1.8
Other	453	23.5	286	7.8	631	−15.7
Totals	1,937	100.0	3,657	100.0	1,888	

Sources: Système d'observation permanente des migrations, *1978 Report* (Paris: Organization of Economic and Community Development, 1979), p. 3, and *Handelsblatt*, June 1, 1978.

Note: $1 = 1.75 DM.

tion, which undercuts the purchasing power of the nonremittance-receiving population. Moreover when such money is spent on imported consumer goods, the balance-of-payments deficits between emigrant-sending and -receiving societies are thrown out of balance.

Another problem is that labor-sending societies often fail to prevent skilled workers from emigrating to labor-receiving societies. Consequently regional shortages of skilled labor necessary to effect development plans or simply to maintain existing regional economies arise. Also skilled emigrant workers proved to be the least likely to return, thereby thwarting hopes that emigration policies would produce skilled workers who would return and contribute to economic development. Pay differentials and the nontransferability of skills to emigrant-sending societies resulted in the loss of some of the most dynamic portions of emigrant-sending society work forces to the advance industrial societies of Western Europe.

The readjustment of returning migrants to source-society economies has been an especially acute problem, for it was not uncommon for them to remain unemployed for several years upon their return home.[6] In part, these former emigrants were taking extended vacations or were content to live off their savings upon return. However, in many other cases, unemployed foreign workers returned home and were unable to find employment in their native societies, which were poorly equipped to absorb the some 2 million migrant workers who returned home in the wake of the recruitment halts in Western Europe. These return flows aggravated still serious underemployment problems in the labor-sending societies.[7]

Social Consequences

The employment problems of returning migrants resulted in part from a more general social problem: the difficulty of migrant readaptation to labor-sending societies. Foreign workers and their dependents, especially those from rural areas with traditional societal structures and mores, frequently experienced a cultural shock upon arriving in Western Europe. Their disorientation and inability to adapt often resulted in depression, anxiety, and in more severe cases, physical illness.

Despite the tendency of foreign workers to create homeland microcosms in the host societies, they are influenced or socialized by the host-society environment. This is particularly true of foreign-worker children who may have Turkish or Algerian citizenship but have never been in those countries.

Although the emigrant-sending governments attempt to maintain emigrant cultural identity through sponsorship of schools or cultural associations, many foreign workers and their dependents undergo a socialization process that leaves them feeling part of neither the host nor the sending society. Thus when they return home, they have difficulty readjusting. Former villagers may spurn village life and move to cities, sometimes leaving fields to lie fallow while not finding work in the cities. They may be culturally alienated from traditional mores or encounter problems of familial readjustment after years of separation. The psychological toll of separation from family and friends is exacted not only on the emigrants but also on those who remain behind. Wives and children of migrant workers frequently suffer from depression. Juvenile delinquency among migrant children is almost as much a problem in the homelands as it is in the European host societies.

In a recent study of the effects of migrant-labor policy upon Greece, Demetrios Papademetriou succinctly described the social costs of emigration to one society but this description fits other emigrant-sending societies as well:

> At the most general level, the human costs of emigration are staggering. Emigration is directly responsible for a multitude of sociopsychological traumas and for the creation of a class of sociocultural pariahs who live suspended between two cultures, leading a marginal existence at the fringes of both societies. This "dehumanization" of the migrants commences at the time of their initial application for emigration and frequently lasts until well after they have returned to Greece. It is responsible for the alienation, cynicism, and hostility observed among many foreign workers. This "dehumanization" is further compounded by serious problems of family disruption and disintegration, by the sociocultural consequences of frequent changes in family power structure, norms, and general ethos, and by neglect of dependents.[8]

The social costs of emigration to homeland societies often are intangible but they are real. Nonetheless, individual migrants chose to go abroad, and one might argue that the social inconveniences occasioned by migration must be less important than the economic and other benefits derived if migrants continue to go to Western Europe either as dependents or illegals. Many migrants had exaggerated notions of foreign-worker life in Western Europe, due in part to accounts from returning migrants, and once in Europe found it difficult to return due to the continuing lack of jobs and housing in their native societies and the socialization they underwent in the new society.

Political Consequences

Labor emigration usually is seen as being devoid of significant political consequences but sometimes is considered a factor that stabilizes or reinforces the political status quo in an emigrant-sending country. This conclusion follows from the fact that labor emigration relieves unemployment pressure and allows some workers a chance for socioeconomic advancement abroad that they may not have had at home. The image of labor emigration in this case is one of a political safety valve that helps to dissipate social forces that might be mobilized against a government.

There is little, if any, evidence that a political rationale was attached to labor migration to Western Europe other than that multilateral and bilateral labor treaties were seen as fostering good diplomatic relations. However, labor migration has had political consequences upon the sending societies, and there are some indications that labor migration to Western Europe may not have been uniformly stabilizing in terms of domestic homeland politics just as at times labor-migration issues have disrupted rather than promoted foreign relations.

Foreign workers in Western Europe have considerable rights and freedoms of political significance even if they are denied the right to vote. And in spite of the obligation to maintain political neutrality in France and not to disrupt societal order and foreign relations in Germany and Switzerland, foreign workers often are freer to express themselves politically abroad than they are at home. This was more generally true prior to the recent return of Greece and Spain to democratic institutions and the revolution that toppled the Portuguese dictatorship in 1974. Consequently migrant workers continue to participate in various facets of homeland politics while abroad. This participation ranges from membership in politically oriented associations and parties to voting in homeland elections or joining in demonstrations against events in the homeland. In some instances, mainly involving Turks, but also Yugoslavs and North Africans, homeland political rivalries and passions have spilled over to emigrant-worker communities, and deaths have resulted. The series of assassinations perpetrated by the neofascist Turkish Grey Wolf organization against Turkish leftists in Germany constitutes perhaps the most sanguinary example of the tendency for domestic political violence in the homelands to spill over to the labor-receiving countries of Western Europe. There are an estimated 50,000 Turkish political extremists residing in Germany alone, and they are seen as a threat by both Turkey and Germany.

The development of political opposition in the ranks of foreign workers in Western Europe is a concern for most labor-sending governments, including democratic ones. In the case of undemocratic governments, like Morocco and now Turkey, political opponents often are more able to seek support among compatriots abroad than at home. While the various homeland governments attempt to maintain the political support of emigrant workers primarily through consulates and government-controlled fraternal and cultural associations, virtually every major foreign-work nationality group in Western Europe contains opposition parties.

Political opposition in the ranks of migrants may be clandestine or open, largely depending on the nature of the homeland regime. The Italian Communist party (PCI), for example, long has had a solid base of support among Italian emigrants working in Western Europe. The large numbers of Italian foreign workers who return home to vote have proved to be a boon to the the PCIs electoral strength in the past.[9] In the Moroccan case, despite a certain recent democratization, opposition in the ranks of emigrants tends to be clandestine. The Association of Moroccans in France and other opposition groups may open offices, but they generally are underground. Alleged Moroccan police surveillance in France is one reason for this. Each summer, scores of vacationing Moroccan emigrant workers are jailed for membership in organizations like the CGT, a trade union dominated by the French Communist party.[10]

While there are discernible blocs of pro-status-quo and anti-status-quo political forces among emigrant workers, it is difficult to tell whether this has significantly affected emigrant-country political systems and in what manner. Despite the PCI's strength in the Italian emigrant-worker community, this opposition from abroad has not significantly altered power structures in southern Italy from where most of the migrants come. However, emigrant-worker politicization through trade union or associational ties in Western Europe already seems to have had some effect upon left-leaning trade union movements in Turkey, Morocco and Tunisia. It seems plausible that the combination of heightened expectations as a result of emigration and a certain radicalization undergone by some migrants could be long-term destabilizing influences in several of the Mediterranean basin countries.

Notes

1. André Lebon, "Les transfers de fonds des travailleurs étrangers," in Société française pour le droit international, ed., *Les travailleurs étrangers et le droit international* (Paris: Editions A. Pedone, 1979), pp. 377-381.

2. Ibid., p. 369.

3. W.R. Böhning, "International Migration in Western Europe: Reflections on the Past Five Years," *International Labor Review* 118 (1979): 409-411.

4. Lebon, *Les transfers de fond des travailleurs étrangers*, p. 368.

5. Stephen Adler, "Emigration and Development in Algeria: Doubts and Dilemmas," (unpublished paper, Conference on Temporary Labour Migration in Europe, Belmont, Maryland:June 1980), p. 25.

6. S. Lieberman and A. Gitmez, "Turkey," in R.E. Krane, ed., *International Labor Migration in Europe*, (New York: Praeger, 1979), p. 215.

7. Böhning, "International Migration," p. 404.

8. Demetrios Papedemetriou, "Greece," in Krane, *International Labor Migration*, p. 193.

9. André Vieuguet, *Français et Immigrés* (Paris: Editions Sociales, 1975), p. 186.

10. Comité de lutte contre la répression au Maroc, *Maroc: Répression, prison, emigration* (n.d.).

10 Lessons for the United States

The postwar Western European experience with foreign workers suggests potential problems, likely consequences, and administrative options associated with foreign-worker policy in Western democracies. It constitutes a particularly instructive background for consideration of the desirability of expanding U.S. foreign-worker policy and the administrative contours of that policy if expansion is deemed desirable. Perhaps the most important lesson to be learned from the Western European experience is the need to take a comprehensive view of foreign-worker policy in order to anticipate and resolve issues before launching a large-scale program.

The lessons to be derived from Western Europe in the foreign-worker policy area can be broken down into four categories: economic, administrative, sociopolitical, and foreign policy. This categorization, however, should not obscure a second general lesson to be drawn from Western Europe: foreign-worker policy is a chain of components whose administrative, economic, social, and foreign-policy dimensions are inextricably linked rather than discrete. Hence there is a need for comprehensive planning through an instrument, such as a national advisory council, that brings together local, state, and federal officials with representatives of labor, business, religious, and civil-rights organizations. If appropriate, representatives from labor-sending countries or perhaps of the migrants themselves also might be included. The goals of this council would be to generate the greatest possible degree of consensus on the shape of an expanded foreign-worker program and to facilitate overall policy coordination.

Economic Lessons

The issue of which jobs shall be opened up to foreign-worker employment must be resolved before program expansion. Under present international norms, foreign workers employed in jobs of a temporary nature may be required to repatriate. Those employed in jobs of a permanent nature are not required to repatriate against their will. If foreign workers are to be employed in jobs of a permanent nature, they should be given the possibility of eventual U.S. citizenship. The temporary-permanent job distinction must be clarified and the overall foreign-worker policy shaped accordingly or the United States will risk international criticism, particularly from the ILO.

103

An expanded foreign-worker policy will tend to foster a dual labor market. Unless foreign workers are not restricted to certain kinds of work, which would seem politically infeasible and in which case migrants presumably could take jobs of a permanent nature, certain jobs will be designated as open to foreign-worker employment. In these job areas, wages and working conditions are likely to decline unless always controversial, adverse-effect controls are introduced. Adverse-effect regulations currently apply to the employment of the United States' 30,000 or so H-2 nonimmigrant workers. Department of Labor determinations of when labor shortages permitting employer recourse to alien labor occur and how much foreign workers should be paid inevitably spark criticism. Employers consistently complain of labor shortages to justify further hiring of alien workers while worker representatives complain that American workers are displaced by H-2 workers and that employers would find ample American labor if they paid decent wages and improved working conditions. Even with controls, a large-scale foreign-worker program might reinforce a two-tiered labor market, with foreign workers disproportionally occupying the least-desirable jobs.

In time, U.S. citizens may reject jobs associated with foreign workers as socially demeaning and thereby create a certain labor-market dependency upon foreign labor. In Western Europe, foreign workers became an indispensable labor-market component in part because of the sheer mass of their numbers but also because native workers came to shun many of the jobs foreigners generally held. A related problem is the proclivity of employers to prefer foreign workers over indigenous workers because the former are less conscious of their rights and less likely to unionize. As a general rule, it is easier to introduce foreign workers into an economy than to replace them with indigenous workers due to the social stigma that comes to be attached to jobs characteristically held by migrants.

Foreign workers may contribute to economic dualism in labor-importing countries. Labor-intensive industries, heavily dependent on migrant labor that would be more appropriately located in developing countries, coexist with high-technology, capital-intensive industries which will increasingly characterize advanced industrial democracies in the future. The availability of foreign workers discourages industrial restructuring by preserving some industries that might otherwise disappear. An example is the European textile industry. Consequently the presence of migrants may preserve the jobs and profits of domestic workers and entrepreneurs but also make it politically necessary to shelter some industries from international competition. The result can be a cleavage between technologically advanced, internationally competitive industries and lagging industries, with very different competitive capacities in international markets.

Within an industry, foreign workers may provoke economic dualism if they are used only by some firms. The firms relying on domestic workers typically use more capital and pay higher wages than those using foreign workers. The result may be two firms producing the identical good or service at the same market price but under very different production arrangements. The economic outcome to consumers is the same, but the human costs of production are very different.

Foreign workers are a subsidy to their employers. By saving employers the costs of job restructuring or rationalization, foreign workers increase employer profits. Employers usually face labor shortages on the lower-wage rungs of the job ladder. In order to fill these jobs with resident workers, employers might have to raise all wages to maintain existing intervals in the wage hierarchy, not just bottom-level wages. If foreign workers are willing to work at existing wages, employers save restructuring costs, thereby increasing profits.

Foreign workers typically save money at significantly higher rates than do citizens. Since foreign workers are producing far more than they consume while abroad, inflationary pressures are reduced. Thus foreign workers swell the labor supply and reduce upward pressure on wages.

Typically foreign workers are youthful and ablebodied in comparison to the citizen population and have a much higher labor-force participation rate, especially in the early stages of labor migration. As a result, foreign workers pay more into pension and social security systems than they withdraw, thereby lessening the burden of supporting retired persons. Further, unless accompanied by dependents and allowed access to public services, foreign workers require relatively few social-infrastructure investments, such as schools, public housing, and hospitals.

If, however, foreign workers and their dependents become eligible for payroll tax benefits as is the case in Western Europe, they may eventually become a net drain on these systems since they might draw proportionally more in benefits than they paid in taxes. Currently there is no incontrovertible evidence that foreign populations have burdened Western European social-welfare systems, but this prospect is widely feared. If foreigners are integrated, they require special public expenditures, particularly for language and vocational training. The benefits derived from the characteristically youthful and ablebodied foreign workers currently are the object of international discussions concerning compensation.

Despite their willingness to work overtime and on unpopular work shifts, a contributing factor to their high accident rates, foreign workers usually earn less than the average citizen worker (between 5 an 10 percent less in Western Europe). Since foreign workers add to the bottom half of income distribution, overall income inequality increases.

The availability of foreign workers may discourage capital investment, especially in times of economic uncertainty. Their availability also holds down general wage levels, thus discouraging labor-saving capital investments. If employers argue that they cannot operate without low-cost foreign labor, they are really saying that consumers will not buy their goods or services unless government intervenes to provide a subsidy—in this case a wage subsidy.

In most nations, the cost of idle capital is borne solely by the owner, but the cost of idle workers is shared by all employers (in the form of unemployment insurance) or by society at large (in the form of welfare). If business cannot predict future demands for its products, managers tend to maximize their variable costs (those that stop when production ceases). An employer who faces the choice between a labor-saving capital investment, whose interest payments must be made even if the machine is idle, and extra workers will choose additional workers if he or she is uncertain about the future. Foreign workers encourage this labor-intensive choice in two ways. Their availability gives the employer the labor option, and the fact that they are foreign lends general credence to the notion that the costs of supporting them when idle can be shifted to the sending countries. Despite sending-country protests, this belief that the burden of unemployment can be shifted abroad persists in labor-importing nations.

Administrative Lessons

Foreign-worker policy will attenuate, not end, illegal immigration. In Western Europe, an illegal-alien population conservatively estimated at 10 percent of the total legal-alien population has developed over the postwar period despite large-scale legal employment opportunities for foreigners. Illegal-alien inflows may be generated by migrant-worker programs as aspiring foreign workers seek to avoid administrative delays or emigrate illegally after not being selected for coveted work opportunities abroad. Increasingly severe European penalties for the trafficking and employment of illegal aliens combined with national identity card systems that allow the police to demand identification of both citizens and legally resident aliens have, however, been instrumental in curbing illegal immigration. An expanded American foreign-worker policy not accompanied by employer sanctions, a mandatory identity card system, and enforcement would run a strong risk of not significantly reducing illegal-alien employment.

A large fraction of foreign workers will not voluntarily repatriate. Western European foreign-worker policies, with a few exceptions, were based on the assumption that foreign workers would repatriate. This assumption was partially based on surveys indicating that most migrants wanted to return home after relatively short stays abroad. Actual voluntary return rates varied considerably by nationality group, but only seasonal workers, plus some unemployed foreigners, were forced to return home. Based on the Western European experience, it would seem imprudent to build an American foreign-worker policy on surveys of foreign workers' intentions or expectations of short-term sojourns. Unless required to return, a sizable fraction of foreign workers probably will choose to stay on, and, under prevailing international norms, foreign workers admitted for permanent-type employment cannot be forced to leave. Inducements to return, such as cash bonuses, are expensive and unlikely to ensure return. In Western Europe, a combination of diplomatic engagements and lack of attention paid to the question of return has resulted in foreign-worker policies becoming de facto immigration policies.

Long-term foreign workers eventually will be joined by family members. According to international norms, foreign workers admitted to perform work of a nontemporary character should be allowed to bring in their families after a one-year delay. Only seasonal workers employed in jobs of a temporary character can be denied family-entry rights. Seasonal worker dependents, through, should be granted visiting rights.

In Western Europe, long-term foreign workers increasingly have been joined by family members. Seasonal worker dependents have been a major source of illegal alien entry and residency in Switzerland. Legal family entry might be curtailed by recruiting only unmarried foreign workers for seasonal employment. However, these workers would seem the most likely to violate mandatory return requirements because they would not have dependents to whom to return. Such a policy would heighten the social isolation of migrant workers.

Foreign workers of various nationalities should be granted similar status because variable foreign-worker statutes complicate the administration of foreign-worker policy. Moreover, disfavored foreign workers and their governments resent their inferior status, which adds to social and political tensions within the host nation and between the host and sending nations.

Anonymous-type recruitment enables labor-sending countries to exert more control over recruitment, thereby making emigrant labor policy more responsive to their developmental needs. This style of recruitment permits the emigrant-sending state, with the approval of receiving-country officials, to match a worker to a job rather than having an employer do it, a system that tends to cut down losses of skilled or educated workers to the host society.

Recruitment should be government controlled as opposed to direct employer recruitment. This arrangement facilitates vital intergovernmental cooperation and would be more in line with the provisions of various ILO instruments. Direct employer recruitment, such as practiced in Switzerland, however, is in conformity with the instruments as long as employers adhere to certain guidelines. One drawback to state-operated recruitment is the opportunity it creates for corruption or manipulation of recruitment to favor political friends.

Sociopolitical Lessons

Foreign-worker programs are inherently discriminatory because foreign-worker rights are limited as compared with those of citizens. This discrimination is incompatible with the democratic ideal of equality of treatment and opportunity. While foreign workers have more rights and protections than do illegal aliens, a foreign-worker policy publicly sanctions the creation of a disadvantaged minority, which, in spite of official safeguards, is still prone to discrimination and exploitation. The responsibility of a government in safeguarding the rights of alien workers is much greater when they are legal foreign workers.

The underprivileged status of foreign workers is likely to become the object of human and civil-rights-type campaigns, which, if successful, might make foreign-worker repatriation politically impossible. Further, xenophobic reactions to foreign workers radicalize domestic politics of host nations as extremist movements of the left and right seek to mobilize support on the issue.

Foreign-worker policy diminishes the quality of democratic life. As noncitizens, foreign workers cannot vote in regular elections, accentuating the problem of nonparticipation in democratic institutions. Further, political parties responsive to working-class constituencies feel disadvantaged by the disenfranchisement of foreign workers who are considered natural supporters of such parties.

Despite their noncitizen status, foreign workers can have a significant nonelectoral political impact, especially upon trade unions, progressive political parties, and civil rights-civil liberties organizations. Their participation in homeland politics can complicate foreign policy and may give rise to reciprocal feelings of interference in domestic affairs.

Foreign-Policy Lessons

Foreign-worker policy may not be mutually beneficial to the labor-sending and labor-receiving nations. Ideally from the perspective of labor-sending countries, foreign-worker policy relieves unemployment and attendant sociopolitical stress, provides needed remittances, and enables migrants to learn skills transferable to the homeland. These positive outcomes, however, are mitigated by the situation of dependency fostered by reliance upon another country to provide employment and remittances. The provision of workers to another country usually is seen as a temporary measure that will accelerate development. In time, this development should reduce the economic problems that gave rise to the need to export workers in the first place.

This expectation has yet to be realized by any significant labor-sending partner in foreign-worker policy. Instead chronic unemployment remains, as do developmental disparities. Indeed participation in foreign-worker policy may forestall structural reforms necessary for development. Emigrant remittances have not been a major source of development capital. Rather they tend to be spent on consumer goods, which in turn worsens trade deficits and balance-of-payments problems. While remittances are the sustenance of many foreign-worker dependents, they are a mixed blessing for the homelands. Abrupt declines in the inflow of remittances can serious ly aggravate socioeconomic problems at times when governments are the least prepared to cope with the loss. Labor emigration has disruptive effects upon agriculture in many homelands. Vital farm work is neglected with sometimes permanent damage being done to delicate irrigation systems. The resultant loss of agricultural production may necessitate compensatory imports of foodstuffs.

A foreign-worker policy also has not met expectations concerning migrants obtaining skills beneficial to the homelands. In fact, homelands frequently experience a loss of needed skilled workers through their participation in foreign-worker programs. Skilled migrants are the least likely to return and, if they do, they often find that their skills are not those needed by the homeland. Moreover, many homelands have been disappointed by host-society shortcomings in training migrants.

Increasingly homeland societies are reassessing the benefits of foreign-worker policy. Homeland societies pay for the upbringing and early education of migrants, only to see them spend part or even most of their productive years contributing mainly to the economic development of another nation. There is some feeling that foreign-worker policy actually increases the gap between industrial and the lesser-developed countries, thereby perpetuating conditions that push workers to migrate. There also is increasing awareness of the social disruption and personal hardship (for example, families being broken up and juvenile delinquency) brought on by labor emigration.

Foreign-worker policy does not necessarily ameliorate bilateral relations with emigration countries. In addition to long-term economic grievances, foreign-worker policy has potential diplomatic pitfalls. Labor emigration greatly increases the scope of intersocietal contacts, which may have a beneficial effect upon bilateral relations, however, incidents involving foreign workers, especially violent crimes committed against them, will have a deleterious impact on bilateral relations. The breadth of intersocietal contacts fostered by foreign workers lessens the ability of governments to control foreign policy. For example, if significant political opposition to a homeland government develops among the ranks of foreign workers, foreign-worker activities are likely to complicate bilateral relations. If host-society governments are not successful in enforcing safeguards on behalf of emigrants, bilateral relations are likely to suffer despite the best intentions of the host-society government. Homeland governments tend to be nationalistic and sensitive to real or alleged mistreatment of emigrant citizens. Apparently minor incidents can mushroom into crises, especially if the emigrant-sending government must contend with significant opposition to participation in bilateral labor programs.

Foreign-worker policy does not necessarily reinforce sociopolitical stability in the homeland. Relief of unemployment pressure and attendant stress is mitigated by a parallel destabilizing revolution in expectations. Uprooted migrants often undergo fundamental transformation of their way of life, and generally their aspirations are heightened. The problem of popular aspirations exceeding the ability of governments to keep pace has been identified as a key factor giving rise to political instability in modernizing countries.

Foreign-worker policy increasingly is subject to international scrutiny. Such policy must conform to international expectations or risk becoming a human-rights issue. The guidelines of international organizations favor migrant rights and oppose the notion of forcible repatriation for migrants employed in jobs of a permanent character. Hence it would be difficult to enforce nonseasonal migrant return without some criticism from the international community. The diplomatically sensitive nature of foreign-worker policy recommends close adhesion to the various ILO instruments on migrant workers.

Labor migration could be the cure for labor shortages in industrial societies and unemployment in developing countries. But European experience shows that there is nothing in the labor-migration process that automatically assures mutual benefits. Instead European experience urges caution, warning that unanticipated consequences are the rule, not the exception.

Guest workers benefit themselves and their employers. But costs inevitably follow, costs that are borne by whole societies, not just the benefiting participants. The fundamental caution of guest workers is this distributional one: guest workers benefit one domestic group at one time but later impose socioeconomic costs on everyone. The industrial societies that hold the key to labor transfers may still elect to organize or sanction migrant labor, but they can no longer protest that they innocently opened a Pandora's box.

**Appendix A:
Current Western
European Labor-
Certification
Procedures for Foreign-
Worker Employment**

Appendix A

	France (pre-1980)		Switzerland (pre-1980)		Federal Republic of Germany	
	Initial	Renewal of Permit	Initial	Renewal of Permit	Initial	Renewal of Permit
Employer must seek authorization	Yes	Yes	Yes	Yes	Yes	Yes
Job offer must conform to standard wages	Yes	Yes	Yes	Yes	Yes	Yes
Appropriate wages determined by collective wage rate agreements	Infrequently	Infrequently	Yes	Yes	Yes	Yes
Minimum wage	Yes	Yes	No	No	No	No
Adequate-housing provision	Yes	Yes	Yes	Yes	Yes	Yes
Prescribed waiting period before foreigner may satisfy job offer	Yes[a]	N/A	Yes[g]	Variable[j] (seasonal 3 mos.)	Yes[a]	N/A
Employment request routinely circulated through employment agencies	Yes[b]	N/A	Yes[h]	N/A	Yes[m]	Yes[m]
Employer must advertise offer in newpaper	May be required	N/A	May be required	N/A	May be required	N/A
Indigenous worker priority	Yes	Yes	Yes	Yes	Yes	Yes
Indigenous worker definition includes some foreign workers	Yes[d]	Yes[d]	Yes[i]	Yes[i]	Yes[n]	Yes[n]
Pro forma labor-market tests in periods of low unemployment	Yes	Yes	Yes	Yes	Yes	Yes
Informal blanket certification in low-skilled, socially undesirable jobs in periods of low unemployment	Yes	Yes	Yes	Yes	Yes	Yes
Authorization curtailed in periods of high unemployment (except some highly skilled categories)	Yes	Somewhat	Yes	Somewhat	Yes	Somewhat
Health, crime, and political criteria apply	Yes	Yes	Yes	Yes	Yes	Yes
Authorization quotas by economic sectors	Pro forma	Pro forma[e]	In some cases	In some cases	No	No
Seasonal-worker quotas	No	N/A	Yes	N/A	No	No
National quota system	No	No	Yes	Yes[k]	No	No

	Portugal Algeria				South Korea Morroco Tunisia	
Bilateral quotas	Portugal Algeria	N/A	No	No	South Korea Morroco Tunisia	N/A
Sanctions against illegal-alien employment	Yes	Yes	Yes	Yes	Yes	Yes
Employer legal recourse if authorization is denied	Yes	Yes	Yes	Yes	Yes	Yes
Limited exceptions made to 1973-1974 recruitment bans	Yes	N/A	Yes[e]	N/A[l]	Yes	N/A
Possibility of ex-post-facto authorization (adjustment of status)	No[f]	N/A	No[f]	N/A	No	N/A

[a] Eighteen days for EEC search.
[b] Locally.
[c] Not in all jobs.
[d] Permit C and EEC.
[e] Law of 1932 abrogated in 1979.
[f] In principle.
[g] Variable by permit; usually two to three weeks.
[h] Cantonal level on by.
[i] Certificate C and annuals with five years of residency.
[j] Seasonal three months.
[k] Annuals and seasonals.
[l] OFIAMT contingent and seasonal.
[m] Quasi-national.
[n] EEC and foreigners with five years of residency.

**Appendix B:
Texts of Principal
ILO Instruments
concerning Migrant
Workers**

CONVENTION (No. 97) CONCERNING MIGRATION FOR EMPLOYMENT (REVISED 1949)

The General Conference of the International Labour Organisation,

Having been convened at Geneva by the Governing Body of the International Labour Office, and having met in its Thirty-second Session on 8 June 1949, and

Having decided upon the adoption of certain proposals with regard to the revision of the Migration for Employment Convention, 1939, adopted by the Conference at its Twenty-fifth Session, which is included in the eleventh item on the agenda of the session, and

Considering that these proposals must take the form of an international Convention,

adopts this first day of July of the year one thousand nine hundred and forty-nine the following Convention, which may be cited as the Migration for Employment Convention (Revised), 1949 :

Article 1

Each Member of the International Labour Organisation for which this Convention is in force undertakes to make available on request to the International Labour Office and to other Members—

(a) information on national policies, laws and regulations relating to emigration and immigration ;

(b) information on special provisions concerning migration for employment and the conditions of work and livelihood of migrants for employment ;

(c) information concerning general agreements and special arrangements on these questions concluded by the Member.

Article 2

Each Member for which this Convention is in force undertakes to maintain, or satisfy itself that there is maintained, an adequate and free service to assist migrants for employment, and in particular to provide them with accurate information.

Article 3

1. Each Member for which this Convention is in force undertakes that it will, so far as national laws and regulations permit.

ILO Instruments pertaining to Migrant Workers, *Convention 97* (1949). Reprinted with permission.

take all appropriate steps against misleading propaganda relating to emigration and immigration.

2. For this purpose it will where appropriate act in co-operation with other Members concerned.

Article 4

Measures shall be taken as appropriate by each Member, within its jurisdiction, to facilitate the departure, journey and reception of migrants for employment.

Article 5

Each Member for which this Convention is in force undertakes to maintain, within its jurisdiction, appropriate medical services responsible for—

(a) ascertaining, where necessary, both at the time of departure and on arrival, that migrants for employment and the members of their families authorised to accompany or join them are in reasonable health ;

(b) ensuring that migrants for employment and members of their families enjoy adequate medical attention and good hygienic conditions at the time of departure, during the journey and on arrival in the territory of destination.

Article 6

1. Each Member for which this Convention is in force undertakes to apply, without discrimination in respect of nationality, race, religion or sex, to immigrants lawfully within its territory, treatment no less favourable than that which it applies to its own nationals in respect of the following matters :

(a) in so far as such matters are regulated by law or regulations, or are subject to the control of administrative authorities—

(i) remuneration, including family allowances where these form part of remuneration, hours of work, overtime arrangements, holidays with pay, restrictions on home work, minimum age for employment, apprenticeship and training, women's work and the work of young persons ;

(ii) membership of trade unions and enjoyment of the benefits of collective bargaining ;

(iii) accommodation ;

(b) social security (that is to say, legal provision in respect of employment injury, maternity, sickness, invalidity, old age, death, unemployment and family responsibilities, and any other contingency which, according to national laws or regulations, is covered by a social security scheme), subject to the following limitations :

(i) there may be appropriate arrangements for the maintenance of acquired rights and rights in course of acquisition ;

(ii) national laws or regulations of immigration countries may prescribe special arrangements concerning benefits or portions of benefits which are payable wholly out of public funds, and concerning allowances paid to persons who do not fulfil the contribution conditions prescribed for the award of a normal pension ;

(c) employment taxes, dues or contributions payable in respect of the person employed ; and

(d) legal proceedings relating to the matters referred to in this Convention.

2. In the case of a federal State the provisions of this Article shall apply in so far as the matters dealt with are regulated by federal law or regulations or are subject to the control of federal administrative authorities. The extent to which and manner in which these provisions shall be applied in respect of matters regulated by the law or regulations of the constituent States, provinces or cantons, or subject to the control of the administrative authorities thereof, shall be determined by each Member. The Member shall indicate in its annual report upon the application of the Convention the extent to which the matters dealt with in this Article are regulated by federal law or regulations or are subject to the control of federal administrative authorities. In respect of matters which are regulated by the law or regulations of the constituent States, provinces or cantons, or are subject to the control of the administrative authorities thereof, the Member shall take the steps provided for in paragraph 7 *(b)* of Article 19 of the Constitution of the International Labour Organisation.

Article 7

1. Each Member for which this Convention is in force undertakes that its employment service and other services connected with migration will co-operate in appropriate cases with the corresponding services of other Members.

2. Each Member for which this Convention is in force undertakes to ensure that the services rendered by its public employment service to migrants for employment are rendered free.

Article 8

1. A migrant for employment who has been admitted on a permanent basis and the members of his family who have been authorised to accompany or join him shall not be returned to their territory of origin or the territory from which they emigrated because the migrant is unable to follow his occupation by reason of illness contracted or injury sustained sub-

sequent to entry, unless the person concerned so desires or an international agreement to which the Member is a party so provides.

2. When migrants for employment are admitted on a permanent basis upon arrival in the country of immigration the competent authority of that country may determine that the provisions of paragraph 1 of this Article shall take effect only after a reasonable period which shall in no case exceed five years from the date of admission of such migrants.

Article 9

Each Member for which this Convention is in force undertakes to permit, taking into account the limits allowed by national laws and regulations concerning export and import of currency, the transfer of such part of the earnings and savings of the migrant for employment as the migrant may desire.

Article 10

In cases where the number of migrants going from the territory of one Member to that of another is sufficiently large, the competent authorities of the territories concerned shall, whenever necessary or desirable, enter into agreements for the purpose of regulating matters of common concern arising in connection with the application of the provisions of this Convention.

Article 11

1. For the purpose of this Convention the term "migrant for employment" means a person who migrates from one country to another with a view to being employed otherwise than on his own account and includes any person regularly admitted as a migrant for employment.

2. This Convention does not apply to—

(a) frontier workers ;

(b) short-term entry of members of the liberal professions and artistes ; and

(c) seamen.

Article 12

The formal ratifications of this Convention shall be communicated to the Director-General of the International Labour Office for registration.

Article 13

1. This Convention shall be binding only upon those Members of the International Labour Organisation whose ratifications have been registered with the Director-General.

2. It shall come into force twelve months after the date on which the ratifications of two Members have been registered with the Director-General.

3. Thereafter, this Convention shall come into force for any Member twelve months after the date on which its ratification has been registered.

Article 14

1. Each Member ratifying this Convention may, by a declaration appended to its ratification, exclude from its ratification any or all of the Annexes to the Convention.

2. Subject to the terms of any such declaration, the provisions of the Annexes shall have the same effect as the provisions of the Convention.

3. Any Member which makes such a declaration may subsequently by a new declaration notify the Director-General that it accepts any or all of the Annexes mentioned in the declaration ; as from the date of the registration of such notification by the Director-General the provisions of such Annexes shall be applicable to the Member in question.

4. While a declaration made under paragraph 1 of this Article remains in force in respect of any Annex, the Member may declare its willingness to accept that Annex as having the force of a Recommendation.

Article 15

1. Declarations communicated to the Director-General of the International Labour Office in accordance with paragraph 2 of Article 35 of the Constitution of the International Labour Organisation shall indicate—

(a) the territories in respect of which the Member concerned undertakes that the provisions of the Convention and any or all of the Annexes shall be applied without modification ;

(b) the territories in respect of which it undertakes that the provisions of the Convention and any or all of the Annexes shall be applied subject to modifications, together with details of the said modifications ;

(c) the territories in respect of which the Convention and any or all of the Annexes, are inapplicable and in such cases the grounds on which they are inapplicable ; and

(d) the territories in respect of which it reserves its decision pending further consideration of the position.

2. The undertakings referred to in subparagraphs (a) and (b) of paragraph 1 of this Article shall be deemed to be an integral part of the ratification and shall have the force of ratification.

3. Any Member may at any time by a subsequent declaration cancel in whole or in part any reservations made in its original declaration in virtue of subparagraphs *(b)*, *(c)* or *(d)* of paragraph 1 of this Article.

4. Any Member may, at any time at which the Convention is subject to denunciation in accordance with the provisions of Article 17, communicate to the Director-General a declaration modifying in any other respect the terms of any former declaration and stating the present position in respect of such territories as it may specify.

Article 16

1. Declarations communicated to the Director-General of the International Labour Office in accordance with paragraphs 4 and 5 of Article 35 of the Constitution of the International Labour Organisation shall indicate whether the provisions of this Convention and any or all of the Annexes will be applied in the territory concerned without modification or subject to modifications ; and if the declaration indicates that the provisions of the Convention and any or all of the Annexes will be applied subject to modifications, it shall give details of the said modifications.

2. The Member, Members or international authority concerned may at any time by a subsequent declaration renounce in whole or in part the right to have recourse to any modification indicated in any former declaration.

3. The Member, Members or international authority concerned may, at any time at which this Convention or any or all of the Annexes are subject to denunciation in accordance with the provisions of Article 17, communicate to the Director-General a declaration modifying in any other respect the terms of any former declaration and stating the present position in respect of the application of the Convention.

Article 17

1. A Member which has ratified this Convention may denounce it after the expiration of ten years from the date on which the Convention first comes into force, by an act communicated to the Director-General of the International Labour Office for registration. Such denunciation shall not take effect until one year after the date on which it is registered.

2. Each Member which has ratified this Convention and which does not, within the year following the expiration of the period of ten years mentioned in the preceding paragraph, exercise the right of denunciation provided for in this Article, will be bound for another period of ten years and, thereafter, may denounce this Convention at the expiration of each period of ten years under the terms provided for in this Article.

3. At any time at which this Convention is subject to denunciation in accordance with the provisions of the preceding paragraphs any Member which does not so denounce it may communicate to the Director-General a declaration denouncing separately any Annex to the Convention which is in force for that Member.

4. The denunciation of this Convention or of any or all of the Annexes shall not affect the rights granted thereunder to a migrant or to the members of his family if he immigrated while the Convention or the relevant Annex was in force in respect of the territory where the question of the continued validity of these rights arises.

Article 18

1. The Director-General of the International Labour Office shall notify all Members of the International Labour Organisation of the registration of all ratifications, declarations and denunciations communicated to him by the Members of the Organisation.

2. When notifying the Members of the Organisation of the registration of the second ratification communicated to him, the Director-General shall draw the attention of the Members of the Organisation to the date upon which the Convention will come into force.

Article 19

The Director-General of the International Labour Office shall communicate to the Secretary-General of the United Nations for registration in accordance with Article 102 of the Charter of the United Nations full particulars of all ratifications, declarations and acts of denunciation registered by him in accordance with the provisions of the preceding articles.

Article 20

At the expiration of each period of ten years after the coming into force of this Convention, the Governing Body of the International Labour Office shall present to the General Conference a report on the working of this Convention and shall consider the desirability of placing on the agenda of the Conference the question of its revision in whole or in part.

Article 21

1. Should the Conference adopt a new Convention revising this Convention in whole or in part, then, unless the new Convention otherwise provides—

(a) the ratification by a Member of the new revising Convention shall *ipso jure* involve the immediate denunciation of this Convention, notwithstanding the provisions of Article 17 above, if and when the new revising Convention shall have come into force ;

(b) as from the date when the new revising Convention comes into force this Convention shall cease to be open to ratification by the Members.

2. This Convention shall in any case remain in force in its actual form and content for those Members which have ratified it but have not ratified the revising Convention.

Article 22

1. The International Labour Conference may, at any session at which the matter is included in its agenda, adopt by a two-thirds majority a revised text of any one or more of the Annexes to this Convention.

2. Each Member for which this Convention is in force shall, within the period of one year, or, in exceptional circumstances, of eighteen months, from the closing of the session of the Conference, submit any such revised text to the authority or authorities within whose competence the matter lies, for the enactment of legislation or other action.

3. Any such revised text shall become effective for each Member for which this Convention is in force on communication by that Member to the Director-General of the International Labour Office of a declaration notifying its acceptance of the revised text.

4. As from the date of the adoption of the revised text of the Annex by the Conference, only the revised text shall be open to acceptance by Members.

Article 23

The English and French versions of the text of this Convention are equally authoritative.

Annex I

RECRUITMENT, PLACING AND CONDITIONS OF LABOUR OF MIGRANTS FOR EMPLOYMENT RECRUITED OTHERWISE THAN UNDER GOVERNMENT-SPONSORED ARRANGEMENTS FOR GROUP TRANSFER

Article 1

This Annex applies to migrants for employment who are recruited otherwise than under Government-sponsored arrangements for group transfer.

Article 2

For the purpose of this Annex—

(a) the term " recruitment " means—

  (i) the engagement of a person in one territory on behalf of an employer in another territory, or

    (ii) the giving of an undertaking to a person in one terri-
tory to provide him with employment in another territory,

together with the making of any arrangements in connection with the operations mentioned in (i) and (ii) including the seeking for and selection of emigrants and the
preparation for departure of the emigrants ;

(b) the term " introduction " means any operations for ensuring or facilitating the arrival in or admission to a territory
of persons who have been recruited within the meaning of
paragraph *(a)* of this Article; and

(c) the term " placing " means any operations for the purpose
of ensuring or facilitating the employment of persons who
have been introduced within the meaning of paragraph *(b)*
of this Article.

Article 3

1. Each Member for which this Annex is in force, the laws
and regulations of which permit the operations of recruitment,
introduction and placing as defined in Article 2, shall regulate
such of the said operations as are permitted by its laws and
regulations in accordance with the provisions of this Article.

2. Subject to the provisions of the following paragraph, the
right to engage in the operations of recruitment, introduction
and placing shall be restricted to—

(a) public employment offices or other public bodies of the
territory in which the operations take place ;

(b) public bodies of a territory other than that in which the
operations take place which are authorised to operate
in that territory by agreement between the Governments concerned ;

(c) any body established in accordance with the terms of an
international instrument.

3. In so far as national laws and regulations or a bilateral
arrangement permit, the operations of recruitment, introduction and placing may be undertaken by—

(a) the prospective employer or a person in his service acting
on his behalf, subject, if necessary in the interest of the
migrant, to the approval and supervision of the competent
authority ;

(b) a private agency, if given prior authorisation so to do by
the competent authority of the teritory where the said
operations are to take place, in such cases and under such
conditions as may be prescribed by—

    (i)   the laws and regulations of that territory, or

    (ii)   agreement between the competent authority of the
territory of emigration or any body established in
accordance with the terms of an international instru-

ment and the competent authority of the territory of immigration.

4. The competent authority of the territory where the operations take place shall supervise the activities of bodies and persons to whom authorisations have been issued in pursuance of paragraph 3 *(b),* other than any body established in accordance with the terms of an international instrument, the position of which shall continue to be governed by the terms of the said instrument or by any agreement made between the body and the competent authority concerncd.

5. Nothing in this Article shall be deemed to permit the acceptance of a migrant for employment for admission to the territory of any Member by any person or body other than the competent authority of the territory of immigration.

Article 4

Each Member for which this Annex is in force undertakes to ensure that the services rendered by its public employment service in connection with the recruitment, introduction or placing of migrants for employment are rendered free.

Article 5

1. Each Member for which this Annex is in force which maintains a system of supervision of contracts of employment between an employer, or a person acting on his behalf, and a migrant for employment undertakes to require—

(a) that a copy of the contract of employment shall be delivered to the migrant before departure or, if the Governments concerned so agree, in a reception centre on arrival in the territory of immigration ;

(b) that the contract shall contain provisions indicating the conditions of work and particularly the remuneration offered to the migrant ;

(c) that the migrant shall receive in writing before departure, by a document which relates either to him individually or to a group of migrants of which he is a member, information concerning the general conditions of life and work applicable to him in the territory of immigration.

2. Where a copy of the contract is to be delivered to the migrant on arrival in the territory of immigration, he shall be informed in writing before departure, by a document which relates either to him individually or to a group of migrants of which he is a member, of the occupational category for which he is engaged and the other conditions of work, in particular the minimum wage which is guaranteed to him.

3. The competent authority shall ensure that the provisions of the preceding paragraphs are enforced and that appropriate penalties are applied in respect of violations thereof.

Article 6

The measures taken under Article 4 of the Convention shall, as appropriate, include—

(a) the simplification of administrative formalities ;

(b) the provision of interpretation services ;

(c) any necessary assistance during an initial period in the settlement of the migrants and members of their families authorised to accompany or join them ; and

(d) the safeguarding of the welfare, during the journey and in particular on board ship, of migrants and members of their families authorised to accompany or join them.

Article 7

1. In cases where the number of migrants for employment going from the territory of one Member to that of another is sufficiently large, the competent authorities of the territories concerned shall, whenever necessary or desirable, enter into agreements for the purpose of regulating matters of common concern arising in connection with the application of the provisions of this Annex.

2. Where the members maintain a system of supervision over contracts of employment, such agreements shall indicate the methods by which the contractual obligations of the employers shall be enforced.

Article 8

Any person who promotes clandestine or illegal immigration shall be subject to appropriate penalties.

ANNEX II

RECRUITMENT, PLACING AND CONDITIONS OF LABOUR OF MIGRANTS FOR EMPLOYMENT RECRUITED UNDER GOVERNMENT-SPONSORED ARRANGEMENTS FOR GROUP TRANSFER

Article 1

This Annex applies to migrants for employment who are recruited under Government-sponsored arrangements for group transfer.

Article 2

For the purpose of this Annex—

(a) the term " recruitment " means—

    (i) the engagement of a person in one territory on behalf of an employer in another territory under a Government-sponsored arrangement for group transfer, or

(ii)   the giving of an undertaking to a person in one territory to provide him with employment in another territory under a Government-sponsored arrangement for group transfer,

together with the making of any arrangements in connection with the operations mentioned in (i) and (ii) including the seeking for and selection of emigrants and the preparation for departure of the emigrants ;

(b)   the term "introduction" means any operations for ensuring or facilitating the arrival in or admission to a territory of persons who have been recruited under a Government-sponsored arrangement for group transfer within the meaning of subparagraph (a) of this paragraph ; and

(c)   the term "placing" means any operations for the purpose of ensuring or facilitating the employment of persons who have been introduced under a Government-sponsored arrangement for group transfer within the meaning of subparagraph (b) of this paragraph.

Article 3

1.   Each Member for which this Annex is in force, the laws and regulations of which permit the operations of recruitment, introduction and placing as defined in Article 2, shall regulate such of the said operations as are permitted by its laws and regulations in accordance with the provisions of this Article.

2.   Subject to the provisions of the following paragraph, the right to engage in the operations of recruitment, introduction and placing shall be restricted to—

(a)   public employment offices or other public bodies of the territory in which the operations take place ;

(b)   public bodies of a territory other than that in which the operations take place which are authorised to operate in that territory by agreement between the Governments concerned ;

(c)   any body established in accordance with the terms of an international instrument.

3.   In so far as national laws and regulations or a bilateral arrangement permit, and subject, if necessary in the interest of the migrant, to the approval and supervision of the competent authority, the operations of recruitment, introduction and placing may be undertaken by—

(a)   the prospective employer or a person in his service acting on his behalf ;

(b)   private agencies.

4.   The right to engage in the operations of recruitment, introduction and placing shall be subject to the prior authori-

sation of the competent authority of the territory where the said operations are to take place in such cases and under such conditions as may be prescribed by—

(a) the laws and regulations of that territory, or

(b) agreement between the competent authority of the territory of emigration or any body established in accordance with the terms of an international instrument and the competent authority of the territory of immigration.

5. The competent authority of the territory where the operations take place shall, in accordance with any agreements made between the competent authorities concerned, supervise the activities of bodies and persons to whom authorisations have been issued in pursuance of the preceding paragraph, other than any body established in accordance with the terms of an international instrument, the position of which shall continue to be governed by the terms of the said instrument or by any agreement made between the body and the competent authority concerned.

6. Before authorising the introduction of migrants for employment the competent authority of the territory of immigration shall ascertain whether there is not a sufficient number of persons already available capable of doing the work in question.

7. Nothing in this Article shall be deemed to permit the acceptance of a migrant for employment for admission to the territory of any Member by any person or body other than the competent authority of the territory of immigration.

Article 4

1. Each Member for which this Annex is in force undertakes to ensure that the services rendered by its public employment service in connection with the recruitment, introduction or placing of migrants for employment are rendered free.

2. The administrative costs of recruitment, introduction and placing shall not be borne by the migrants.

Article 5

In the case of collective transport of migrants from one country to another necessitating passage in transit through a third country, the competent authority of the territory of transit shall take measures for expediting the passage, to avoid delays and administrative difficulties.

Article 6

1. Each Member for which this Annex is in force which maintains a system of supervision of contracts of employment between an employer, or a person acting on his behalf, and a migrant for employment undertakes to require—

(a) that a copy of the contract of employment shall be delivered to the migrant before departure or, if the Governments concerned so agree, in a reception centre on arrival
in the territory of immigration ;

(b) that the contract shall contain provisions indicating the
conditions of work and particularly the remuneration
offered to the migrant ;

(c) that the migrant shall receive in writing before departure,
by a document which relates either to him individually
or to a group of migrants of which he is a member,
information concerning the general conditions of life and
work applicable to him in the territory of immigration.

2.   Where a copy of the contract is to be delivered to the
migrant on arrival in the territory of immigration, he shall
be informed in writing before departure, by a document which
relates either to him individually or to a group of migrants
of which he is a member, of the occupational category for
which he is engaged and the other conditions of work, in particular the minimum wage which is guaranteed to him.

3.   The competent authority shall ensure that the provisions of the preceding paragraphs are enforced and that appropriate penalties are applied in respect of violations thereof.

Article 7

1.   The measures taken under Article 4 of this Convention
shall, as appropriate, include—

(a) the simplification of administrative formalities ;

(b) the provision of interpretation services ;

(c) any necessary assistance, during an initial period in the
settlement of the migrants and members of their families
authorised to accompany or join them ;

(d) the safeguarding of the welfare, during the journey and
in particular on board ship, of migrants and members
of their families authorised to accompany or join them ;
and

(e) permission for the liquidation and transfer of the property
of migrants for employment admitted on a permanent
basis.

Article 8

Appropriate measures shall be taken by the competent
authority to assist migrants for employment, during an initial
period, in regard to matters concerning their conditions of
employment ; where appropriate, such measures may be taken
in co-operation with approved voluntary organisations.

Article 9

If a migrant for employment introduced into the territory
of a Member in accordance with the provisions of Article 3 of

this Annex fails, for a reason for which he is not responsible, to secure the employement for which he has been recruited or other suitable employment, the cost of his return and that of the members of his family who have been authorised to accompany or join him, including administrative fees, transport and maintenance charges to the final destination, and charges for the transport of household belongings, shall not fall upon the migrant.

Article 10

If the competent authority of the territory of immigration considers that the employment for which a migrant for employment was recruited under Article 3 of this Annex has been found to be unsuitable, it shall take appropriate measures to assist him in finding suitable employment which does not prejudice national workers and shall take such steps as will ensure his maintenance pending placing in such employment, or his return to the area of recruitment if the migrant is willing or agreed to such return at the time of his recruitment, or his resettlement elsewhere.

Article 11

If a migrant for employment who is a refugee or a displaced person and who has entered a territory of immigration in accordance with Article 3 of this Annex becomes redundant in any employment in that territory, the competent authority of that territory shall use its best endeavours to enable him to obtain suitable employment which does not prejudice national workers, and shall take such steps as will ensure his maintenance pending placing in suitable employment or his resettlement elsewhere.

Article 12

1.   The competent authorities of the territories concerned shall enter into agreements for the purpose of regulating matters of common concern arising in connection with the application of the provisions of this Annex.

2.   Where the Members maintain a system of supervision over contracts of employment, such agreements shall indicate the methods by which the contractual obligations of the employer shall be enforced.

 3.   Such agreements shall provide, where appropriate, for co-operation between the competent authority of the territory of emigration or a body established in accordance with the terms of an international instrument and the competent authority of the territory of immigration, in respect of the assistance to be given to migrants concerning their conditions of employment in virtue of the provisions of Article 8.

Article 13

Any person who promotes clandestine or illegal immigration shall be subject to appropriate penalties.

ANNEX III

IMPORTATION OF THE PERSONAL EFFECTS, TOOLS AND EQUIPMENT OF MIGRANTS FOR EMPLOYMENT

Article 1

1. Personal effects belonging to recruited migrants for employment and members of their families who have been authorised to accompany or join them shall be exempt from customs duties on arrival in the territory of immigration.

2. Portable hand-tools and portable equipment of the kind normally owned by workers for the carrying out of their particular trades belonging to recruited migrants for employment and members of their families who have been authorised to accompany or join them shall be exempt from customs duties on arrival in the territory of immigration if such tools and equipment can be shown at the time of importation to be in their actual ownership or possession, to have been in their possession and use for an appreciable time, and to be intended to be used by them in the course of their occupation.

Article 2

1. Personal effects belonging to migrants for employment and members of their families who have been authorised to accompany or join them shall be exempt from customs duties on the return of the said persons to their country of origin if such persons have retained the nationality of that country at the time of their return there.

2. Portable hand-tools and portable equipment of the kind normally owned by workers for the carrying out of their particular trades belonging to migrants for employment and members of their families who have been authorised to accompany or join them shall be exempt from customs duties on return of the said persons to their country of origin if such persons have retained the nationality of that country at the time of their return there and if such tools and equipment can be shown at the time of importation to be in their actual ownership or possession, to have been in their possession and use for an appreciable time, and to be intended to be used by them in the course of their occupation.

Convention 143

CONVENTION CONCERNING MIGRATIONS IN ABUSIVE CONDITIONS AND THE PROMOTION OF EQUALITY OF OPPORTUNITY AND TREATMENT OF MIGRANT WORKERS.

The General Conference of the International Labour Organisation,

Having been convened at Geneva by the Governing Body of the International Labour Office, and having met in its Sixtieth Session on 4 June 1975, and

Considering that the Preamble of the Constitution of the International Labour Organisation assigns to it the task of protecting " the interests of workers when employed in countries other than their own ", and

Considering that the Declaration of Philadelphia reaffirms, among the principles on which the Organisation is based, that " labour is not a commodity ", and that " poverty anywhere constitutes a danger to prosperity everywhere ", and recognises the solemn obligation of the ILO to further programmes which will achieve in particular full employment through " the transfer of labour, including for employment . . .",

Considering the ILO World Employment Programme and the Employment Policy Convention and Recommendation, 1964, and emphasising the need to avoid the excessive and uncontrolled or unassisted increase of migratory movements because of their negative social and human consequences, and

Considering that in order to overcome underdevelopment and structural and chronic unemployment, the governments of many countries increasingly stress the desirability of encouraging the transfer of capital and technology rather than the transfer of workers in accordance with the needs and requests of these countries in the reciprocal interest of the countries of origin and the countries of employment, and

Considering the right of everyone to leave any country, including his own, and to enter his own country, as set forth in the Universal Declaration of Human Rights and the International Covenant on Civil and Political Rights, and

Recalling the provisions contained in the Migration for Employment Convention and Recommendation (Revised), 1949, in the Protection of Migrant Workers (Underdeveloped Countries) Recommendation, 1955, in the Employment Policy Convention and Recommendation, 1964, in the Employment Service Convention and Recommendation, 1948, and in the Fee-Charging Employment Agencies Convention (Revised), 1949, which deal with such matters as the regulation of the recruitment, introduction and placing of migrant workers, the provision of accurate information relating to migration, the minimum conditions to be enjoyed by migrants in transit and on arrival, the adoption of an active employment policy and international collaboration in these matters, and

Considering that the emigration of workers due to conditions in labour markets should take place under the responsibility of official agencies for employment

ILO Instruments pertaining to Migrant Workers, *Recommendation 151* (1975). Reprinted with permission.

or in accordance with the relevant bilateral or multilateral agreements, in particular those permitting free circulation of workers, and

Considering that evidence of the existence of illicit and clandestine trafficking in labour calls for further standards specifically aimed at eliminating these abuses, and

Recalling the provisions of the Migration for Employment Convention (Revised), 1949, which require ratifying Members to apply to immigrants lawfully within their territory treatment not less favourable than that which they apply to their nationals in respect of a variety of matters which it enumerates, in so far as these are regulated by laws or regulations or subject to the control of administrative authorities, and

Recalling that the definition of the term " discrimination " in the Discrimination (Employment and Occupation) Convention, 1958, does not mandatorily include distinctions on the basis of nationality, and

Considering that further standards, covering also social security, are desirable in order to promote equality of opportunity and treatment of migrant workers and, with regard to matters regulated by laws or regulations or subject to the control of administrative authorities, ensure treatment at least equal to that of nationals, and

Noting that, for the full success of action regarding the very varied problems of migrant workers, it is essential that there be close co-operation with the United Nations and other specialised agencies, and

Noting that, in the framing of the following standards, account has been taken of the work of the United Nations and of other specialised agencies and that, with a view to avoiding duplication and to ensuring appropriate co-ordination, there will be continuing co-operation in promoting and securing the application of the standards, and

Having decided upon the adoption of certain proposals with regard to migrant workers, which is the fifth item on the agenda of the session, and

Having determined that these proposals shall take the form of an international Convention supplementing the Migration for Employment Convention (Revised), 1949, and the Discrimination (Employment and Occupation) Convention, 1958,

adopts this twenty-fourth day of June of the year one thousand nine hundred and seventy-five the following Convention, which may be cited as the Migrant Workers (Supplementary Provisions) Convention, 1975:

PART 1. MIGRATIONS IN ABUSIVE CONDITIONS

Article 1

Each Member for which this Convention is in force undertakes to respect the basic human rights of all migrant workers.

Article 2

1. Each Member for which this Convention is in force shall systematically seek to determine whether there are illegally employed migrant workers on its territory and whether there depart from, pass through or arrive in its territory any movements

of migrants for employment in which the migrants are subjected during their journey, on arrival or during their period of residence and employment to conditions contravening relevant international multilateral or bilateral instruments or agreements, or national laws or regulations.

2. The representative organisations of employers and workers shall be fully consulted and enabled to furnish any information in their possession on this subject.

Article 3

Each Member shall adopt all necessary and appropriate measures, both within its jurisdiction and in collaboration with other Members—

(a) to suppress clandestine movements of migrants for employment and illegal employment of migrants, and

(b) against the organisers of illicit or clandestine movements of migrants for employment departing from, passing through or arriving in its territory, and against those who employ workers who have immigrated in illegal conditions,

in order to prevent and to eliminate the abuses referred to in Article 2 of this Convention.

Article 4

In particular, Members shall take such measures as are necessary, at the national and the international level, for systematic contact and exchange of information on the subject with other States, in consultation with representative organisations of employers and workers.

Article 5

One of the purposes of the measures taken under Articles 3 and 4 of this Convention shall be that the authors of manpower trafficking can be prosecuted whatever the country from which they exercise their activities.

Article 6

1. Provision shall be made under national laws or regulations for the effective detection of the illegal employment of migrant workers and for the definition and the application of administrative, civil and penal sanctions, which include imprisonment in their range, in respect of the illegal employment of migrant workers, in respect of the organisation of movements of migrants for employment defined as involving the abuses referred to in Article 2 of this Convention, and in respect of knowing assistance to such movements, whether for profit or otherwise.

2. Where an employer is prosecuted by virtue of the provision made in pursuance of this Article, he shall have the right to furnish proof of his good faith.

Article 7

The representative organisations of employers and workers shall be consulted in regard to the laws and regulations and other measures provided for in this Convention and designed to prevent and eliminate the abuses referred to above, and the possibility of their taking initiatives for this purpose shall be recognised.

Article 8

1. On condition that he has resided legally in the territory for the purpose of employment, the migrant worker shall not be regarded as in an illegal or irregular

situation by the mere fact of the loss of his employment, which shall not in itself imply the withdrawal of his authorisation of residence or, as the case may be, work permit.

2. Accordingly, he shall enjoy equality of treatment with nationals in respect in particular of guarantees of security of employment, the provision of alternative employment, relief work and retraining.

Article 9

1. Without prejudice to measures designed to control movements of migrants for employment by ensuring that migrant workers enter national territory and are admitted to employment in conformity with the relevant laws and regulations, the migrant worker shall, in cases in which these laws and regulations have not been respected and in which his position cannot be regularised, enjoy equality of treatment for himself and his family in respect of rights arising out of past employment as regards remuneration, social security and other benefits.

2. In case of dispute about the rights referred to in the preceding paragraph, the worker shall have the possibility of presenting his case to a competent body, either himself or through a representative.

3. In case of expulsion of the worker or his family, the cost shall not be borne by them.

4. Nothing in this Convention shall prevent Members from giving persons who are illegally residing or working within the country the right to stay and to take up legal employment.

PART II. EQUALITY OF OPPORTUNITY AND TREATMENT

Article 10

Each Member for which the Convention is in force undertakes to declare and pursue a national policy designed to promote and to guarantee, by methods appropriate to national conditions and practice, equality of opportunity and treatment in respect of employment and occupation, of social security, of trade union and cultural rights and of individual and collective freedoms for persons who as migrant workers or as members of their families are lawfully within its territory.

Article 11

1. For the purpose of this Part of this Convention, the term " migrant worker " means a person who migrates or who has migrated from one country to another with a view to being employed otherwise than on his own account and includes any person regularly admitted as a migrant worker.

2. This Part of this Convention does not apply to—

(a) frontier workers;

(b) artistes and members of the liberal professions who have entered the country on a short-term basis;

(c) seamen;

(d) persons coming specifically for purposes of training or education;

(e) employees of organisations or undertakings operating within the territory of a country who have been admitted temporarily to that country at the request of their employer to undertake specific duties or assignments, for a limited and defined period of time, and who are required to leave that country on the completion of their duties or assignments.

Article 12

Each Member shall, by methods appropriate to national conditions and practice—

(a) seek the co-operation of employers' and workers' organisations and other appropriate bodies in promoting the acceptance and observance of the policy provided for in Article 10 of this Convention;

(b) enact such legislation and promote such educational programmes as may be calculated to secure the acceptance and observance of the policy;

(c) take measures, encourage educational programmes and develop other activities aimed at acquainting migrant workers as fully as possible with the policy, with their rights and obligations and with activities designed to give effective assistance to migrant workers in the exercise of their rights and for their protection;

(d) repeal any statutory provisions and modify any administrative instructions or practices which are inconsistent with the policy;

(e) in consultation with representative organisations of employers and workers, formulate and apply a social policy appropriate to national conditions and practice which enables migrant workers and their families to share in advantages enjoyed by its nationals while taking account, without adversely affecting the principle of equality of opportunity and treatment, of such special needs as they may have until they are adapted to the society of the country of employment;

(f) take all steps to assist and encourage the efforts of migrant workers and their families to preserve their national and ethnic identity and their cultural ties with their country of origin, including the possibility for children to be given some knowledge of their mother tongue;

(g) guarantee equality of treatment, with regard to working conditions, for all migrant workers who perform the same activity whatever might be the particular conditions of their employment.

Article 13

1. A Member may take all necessary measures which fall within its competence and collaborate with other Members to facilitate the reunification of the families of all migrant workers legally residing in its territory.

2. The members of the family of the migrant worker to which this Article applies are the spouse and dependent children, father and mother.

Article 14

A Member may—

(a) make the free choice of employment, while assuring migrant workers the right to geographical mobility, subject to the conditions that the migrant worker has resided lawfully in its territory for the purpose of employment for a prescribed period not exceeding two years or, if its laws or regulations provide for contracts for a fixed term of less than two years, that the worker has completed his first work contract;

(b) after appropriate consultation with the representative organisations of employers and workers, make regulations concerning recognition of occupational qualifications acquired outside its territory, including certificates and diplomas;

(c) restrict access to limited categories of employment or functions where this is necessary in the interests of the State.

PART III. FINAL PROVISIONS

Article 15

This Convention does not prevent Members from concluding multilateral or bilateral agreements with a view to resolving problems arising from its application.

Article 16

1. Any Member which ratifies this Convention may, by a declaration appended to its ratification, exclude either Part I or Part II from its acceptance of the Convention.

2. Any Member which has made such a declaration may at any time cancel that declaration by a subsequent declaration.

3. Every Member for which a declaration made under paragraph 1 of this Article is in force shall indicate in its reports upon the application of this Convention the position of its law and practice in regard to the provisions of the Part excluded from its acceptance, the extent to which effect has been given, or is proposed to be given, to the said provision and the reasons for which it has not yet included them in its acceptance of the Convention.

Article 17

The formal ratifications of this Convention shall be communicated to the Director-General of the International Labour Office for registration.

Article 18

1. This Convention shall be binding only upon those Members of the International Labour Organisation whose ratifications have been registered with the Director-General.

2. It shall come into force twelve months after the date on which the ratifications of two Members have been registered with the Director-General.

3. Thereafter, this Convention shall come into force for any Member twelve months after the date on which its ratification has been registered.

Article 19

1. A Member which has ratified this Convention may denounce it after the expiration of ten years from the date on which the Convention first comes into force, by an act communicated to the Director-General of the International Labour Office for registration. Such denunciation shall not take effect until one year after the date on which it is registered.

2. Each Member which has ratified this Convention and which does not, within the year following the expiration of the period of ten years mentioned in the preceding paragraph, exercise the right of denunciation provided for in this Article, will be bound for another period of ten years and, thereafter, may denounce this Convention at the expiration of each period of ten years under the terms provided for in this Article.

Article 20

1. The Director-General of the International Labour Office shall notify all Members of the International Labour Organisation of the registration of all ratifications and denunciations communicated to him by the Members of the Organisation.

2. When notifiying the Members of the Organisation of the registration of the second ratification communicated to him, the Director-General shall draw the attention of the Members of the Organisation to the date upon which the Convention will come into force.

Article 21

The Director-General of the International Labour Office shall communicate to the Secretary-General of the United Nations for registration in accordance with Article 102 of the Charter of the United Nations full particulars of all ratifications and acts of denunciation registered by him in accordance with the provisions of the preceding Articles.

Article 22

At such times as it may consider necessary the Governing Body of the International Labour Office shall present to the General Conference a report on the working of this Convention and shall examine the desirability of placing on the agenda of the Conference the question of its revision in whole or in part.

Article 23

1. Should the Conference adopt a new Convention revising this Convention in whole or in part, then, unless the new Convention otherwise provides—

(a) the ratification by a Member of the new revising Convention shall *ipso jure* involve the immediate denunciation of this Convention, notwithstanding the provisions of Article 19 above, if and when the new revising Convention shall have come into force;

(b) as from the date when the new revising Convention comes into force this Convention shall cease to be open to ratification by the Members.

2. This Convention shall in any case remain in force in its actual form and content for those Members which have ratified it but have not ratified the revising Convention.

Article 24

The English and French versions of the text of this Convention are equally authoritative.

RECOMMENDATION (No. 86) CONCERNING MIGRATION FOR EMPLOYMENT (REVISED 1949)

The General Conference of the International Labour Organisation,

Having been convened at Geneva by the Governing Body of the International Labour Office, and having met in its Thirty-second Session on 8 June 1949, and

Having decided upon the adoption of certain proposals with regard to the revision of the Migration for Employment Recommendation, 1939, and the Migration for Employment (Co-operation between States) Recommendation, 1939, adopted by the Conference at its Twenty-fifth Session, which are included in the eleventh item on the agenda of the session, and

Having determined that these proposals shall take the form of a Recommendation,

adopts this first day of July of the year one thousand nine hundred and forty-nine the following Recommendation, which may be cited as the Migration for Employment Recommendation (Revised), 1949 :

The Conference,

Having adopted the Migration for Employment Convention (Revised), 1949, and

Desiring to supplement its provisions by a Recommendation;

Recommends as follows :

I

1. For the purpose of this Recommendation—

(a) the term " migrant for employment " means a person who migrates from one country to another with a view to being employed otherwise than on his own account and includes any person regularly admitted as a migrant for employment ;

(b) the term " recruitment " means—

(i)   the engagement of a person in one territory on behalf of an employer in another territory, or

(ii) the giving of an undertaking to a person in one territory to provide him with employment in another territory,

---

ILO Instruments pertaining to Migrant Workers, *Recommendation 86* (1949). Reprinted with permission.

together with the making of any arrangements in connection with the operations mentioned in (i) and (ii) including the seeking for and selection of emigrants and the preparation for departure of the emigrants ;

(c)   the term " introduction " means any operations for ensuring or facilitating the arrival in or admission to a territory of persons who have been recruited within the meaning of subparagraph *(b)* ;

(d)   the term " placing " means any operations for the purpose of ensuring or facilitating the employment of persons who have been introduced within the meaning of subparagraph *(c)*.

2.   For the purpose of this Recommendation, references to the Government or competent authority of a territory of emigration should be interpreted as referring, in the case of migrants who are refugees or displaced persons, to any body established in accordance with the terms of an international instrument which may be responsible for the protection of refugees and displaced persons who do not benefit from the protection of any Government.

3.   This Recommendation does not apply to—

(a)   frontier workers ;

(b)   short-term entry of members of the liberal professions and artistes ; and

(c)   seamen.

II

4. (1)   It should be the general policy of Members to develop and utilise all possibilities of employment and for this purpose to facilitate the international distribution of manpower and in particular the movement of manpower from countries which have a surplus of manpower to those countries that have a deficiency.

(2)   The measures taken by each Member should have due regard to the manpower situation in the country and the Government should consult the appropriate organisations of employers and workers on all general questions concerning migration for employment.

III

5. (1)   The free service provided in each country to assist migrants and their families and in particular to provide them with accurate information should be conducted—

(a)   by public authorities ; or

(b)   by one or more voluntary organisations not conducted with a view to profit, approved for the purpose by the public authorities, and subject to the supervision of the said authorities ; or

(c)   partly by the public authorities and partly by one or more voluntary organisations fulfilling the conditions stated in subparagraph *(b)* of this Paragraph.

(2)   The service should advise migrants and their families, in their languages or dialects or at least in a language which they can understand, on matters relating to emigration, immigration, employment and living conditions, including health conditions in the place of destination, return to the country of origin or of emigration, and generally speaking any other question which may be of interest to them in their capacity as migrants.

(3)   The service should provide facilities for migrants and their families with regard to the fulfilment of administrative formalities and other steps to be taken in connection with the return of the migrants to the country of origin or of emigration, should the case arise.

(4)   With a view to facilitating the adaptation of migrants, preparatory courses should, where necessary, be organised to inform the migrants of the general conditions and the methods of work prevailing in the country of immigration, and to instruct them in the language of that country.   The countries of emigration and immigration should mutually agree to organise such courses.

6.   On request, information should be made available by Members to the International Labour Office and to other Members concerning their emigration laws and regulations, including administrative provisions relating to restrictions on emigration and facilities granted to emigrants, and appropriate details concerning the categories of persons wishing to emigrate.

7.   On request, information should be made available by Members to the International Labour Office and to other Members concerning their immigration laws and regulations, including administrative provisions, entry permits where needed, number and occupational qualifications of immigrants desired, laws and regulations affecting admission of migrants to employment, and any special facilities granted to migrants and measures to facilitate their adaptation to the economic and social organisation of the country of immigration.

8.   There should, as far as possible, be a reasonable interval between the publication and the coming into force of any measure altering the conditions on which emigration or immigration or the employment of migrants is permitted in order that these conditions may be notifed in good time to persons who are preparing to emigrate.

9.   Provision should be made for adequate publicity to be given at appropriate stages to the principal measures referred to in the preceding Paragraph, such publicity to be in the languages most commonly known to the migrants.

10. Migration should be facilitated by such measures as may be appropriate—

(a)   to ensure that migrants for employment are provided in case of necessity with adequate accommodation, food and clothing on arrival in the country of immigration ;

(b)   to ensure, where necessary, vocational training so as to enable the migrants for employment to acquire the qualifications required in the country of immigration ;

(c)   to permit, taking into account the limits allowed by national laws and regulations concerning export and import of currency, the transfer of such part of the earnings and savings of migrants for employment as the migrants may desire ;

(d)   to arrange, in the case of permanent migration, for the transfer, where desired, to the country of immigration, of the capital of migrants for employment, within the limits allowed by national laws and regulations concerning export and import of currency ;

(e)   to provide access to schools for migrants and members of their families.

11.   Migrants and the members of their families should be assisted in obtaining access to recreation and welfare facilities, and steps should be taken where necessary to ensure that special facilities are made available during the initial period of settlement in the country of immigration.

12.   In the case of migrants under Government-sponsored arrangements for group transfer, medical assistance should be extended to such migrants in the same manner as provided for nationals.

IV

13.   (1) Where necessary in the interest of the migrant, Members should require that any intermediary who undertakes the recruitment, introduction or placing of migrants for employment on behalf of an employer must obtain a written warrant from the employer, or some other document proving that he is acting on the employer's behalf.

(2)   This document should be drawn up in, or translated into, the official language of the country of emigration and should set forth all necessary particulars concerning the employer, concerning the nature and scope of the recruitment, introduction or placing which the intermediary is to undertake, and concerning the employment offered, including the remuneration.

14.   (1) The technical selection of migrants for employment should be carried out in such a way as to restrict migration as little as possible while ensuring that the migrants are qualified to perform the required work.

(2) Responsibility for such selection should be entrusted—

(a) to official bodies ; or

(b) where appropriate, to private bodies of the territory of immigration duly authorised and, where necessary in the interest of the migrant, supervised by the competent authority of the territory of emigration.

(3) The right to engage in selection should be subject to the prior authorisation of the competent authority of the territory where the said operation takes place, in such cases and under such conditions as may be prescribed by the laws and regulations of that territory, or by agreement between the Government of the territory of emigration and the Government of the territory of immigration.

(4) As far as possible, intending migrants for employment should, before their departure from the territory of emigration, be examined for purposes of occupational and medical selection by a representative of the competent authority of the territory of immigration.

(5) If recruitment takes place on a sufficiently large scale there should be arrangements for close liaison and consultation between the competent authorities of the territories of emigration and immigration concerned.

(6) The operations referred to in the preceding subparagraphs of this Paragraph should be carried out as near as possible to the place where the intending migrant is recruited.

15.   (1) Provision should be made by agreement for authorisation to be granted for a migrant for employment introduced on a permanent basis to be accompanied or joined by the members of his family.

(2) The movement of the members of the family of such a migrant authorised to accompany or join him should be specially facilitated by both the country of emigration and the country of immigration.

(3) For the purposes of this Paragraph, the members of the family of a migrant for employment should include his wife and minor children ; favourable consideration should be given to requests for the inclusion of other members of the family dependent upon the migrant.

V

16.   (1) Migrants for employment authorised to reside in a territory and the members of their families authorised to accompany or join them should as far as possible be admitted to employment in the same conditions as nationals.

(2) In countries in which the employment of migrants is subject to restrictions, these restrictions should as far as possible—

(a) cease to be applied to migrants who have regularly resided in the country for a period, the length of which should not, as a rule, exceed five years ; and

(b) cease to be applied to the wife and children of an age to work who have been authorised to accompany or join the migrant, at the same time as they cease to be applied to the migrant.

17.   In countries where the number of migrants for employment is sufficiently large, the conditions of employment of such workers should be specially supervised, such supervision being undertaken according to circumstances either by a special inspection service or by labour inspectors or other officials specialising in this work.

VI

18.   (1) When a migrant for employment has been regularly admitted to the territory of a Member, the said Member should, as far as possible, refrain from removing such person or the members of his family from its territory on account of his lack of means or the state of the employment market, unless an agreement to this effect has been concluded between the competent authorities of the emigration and immigration territories concerned.

(2) Any such agreement should provide—

(a) that the length of time the said migrant has been in the territory of immigration shall be taken into account and that in principle no migrant shall be removed who has been there for more than five years ;

(b) that the migrant must have exhausted his rights to unemployment insurance benefit ;

(c) that the migrant must have been given reasonable notice so as to give him time, more particularly to dispose of his property ;

(d) that suitable arrangements shall have been made for his transport and that of the members of his family ;

(e) that the necessary arrangements shall have been made to ensure that he and the members of his family are treated in a humane manner ; and

(f) that the costs of the return of the migrant and the members of his family and of the transport of their household belongings to their final destination shall not fall on him.

19.   Appropriate steps should be taken by the authorities of the territories concerned to consult the employers' and workers' organisations concerning the operations of recruitment, introduction and placing of migrants for employment.

VII

20.   When migrants for employment or members of their families who have retained the nationality of their State of origin return there, that country should admit such persons to the benefit of any measures in force for the granting of poor relief and unemployment relief, and for promoting the re-employment of the unemployed, by exempting them from the obligation to comply with any condition as to previous residence or employment in the country or place.

VIII

21.   (1) Members should in appropriate cases supplement the Migration for Employment Convention (Revised), 1949, and the preceding paragraphs of the present Recommendation by bilateral agreements, which should specify the methods of applying the principles set forth in the Convention and in the Recommendation.

(2) In concluding such agreements, Members should take into account the provisions of the Model Agreement annexed to the present Recommendation in framing appropriate clauses for the organisation of migration for employment and the regulation of the conditions of transfer and employment of migrants, including refugees and displaced persons.

ANNEX

Model Agreement on Temporary and Permanent Migration for Employment, including Migration of Refugees and Displaced Persons [1]

ARTICLE 1.   EXCHANGE OF INFORMATION

1.   The competent authority of the territory of immigration shall periodically furnish appropriate information to the competent authority of the territory of emigration [or in the case of refugees and displaced persons, to any body established in accordance with the terms of an international instrument which may be responsible for the protection of refugees and displaced persons who do not benefit from the protection of any Government] concerning—

(a)   legislative and administrative provisions relating to entry, employment, residence and *settlement* of migrant *and of their families* ;

[1] The phrases and passages in italics refer primarily to permanent migration ; those enclosed within square brackets refer solely to migration of refugees and displaced persons.

(b) the number, the categories and the occupational qualifications of the migrants desired ;

(c) the conditions of life and work for the migrants and, in particular, cost of living and minimum wages according to occupational categories and regions of employment, supplementary allowances, if any, nature of employments available, bonus on engagement, if any, social security systems and medical assistance, provisions concerning transport of migrants and of their tools and belongings, housing conditions and provisions for the supply of food and clothing, measures relating to the transfer of the migrants' savings and other sums due in virtue of this Agreement ;

(d) special facilities, if any, for migrants ;

(e) facilities for general education and vocational training for migrants ;

(f) *measures designed to promote rapid adaptation of migrants ;*

(g) *procedure and formalities required for naturalisation.*

2. The competent authority of the territory of emigration [or in the case of refugees and displaced persons, any body established in accordance with the terms of an international instrument which may be responsible for the protection of refugees and displaced persons who do not benefit from the protection of any Government] shall bring this information to the attention of persons or bodies interested.

3. The competent authority of the territory of emigration [or in the case of refugees and displaced persons, any body established in accordance with the terms of an international instrument which may be responsible for the protection of refugees and displaced persons who do not benefit from the protection of any Government] shall periodically furnish appropriate information to the competent authority of the territory of immigration concerning—

(a) legislative and administrative provisions relating to emigration ;

(b) the number and occupational qualifications of intending emigrants, *as well as the composition of their families ;*

(c) the social security system ;

(d) special facilities, if any, for migrants ;

(e) *the environment and living conditions to which migrants are accustomed ;*

(f) *the provisions in force regarding the export of capital.*

4. The competent authority of the territory of immigration shall bring this information to the attention of persons or bodies interested.

5. The information mentioned in paragraphs 1 to 4 above shall also be transmitted by the respective parties to the International Labour Office.

ARTICLE 2. ACTION AGAINST MISLEADING PROPAGANDA

1. The parties agree, with regard to their respective territories, to take all practical steps, so far as national laws and regulations permit, against misleading propaganda relating to emigration and immigration.

2. For this purpose the parties will, where appropriate, act in co-operation with the competent authorities of other countries concerned.

ARTICLE 3. ADMINISTRATIVE FORMALITIES

The parties agree to take measures with a view to accelerating and simplifying the carrying out of administrative formalities relating to departure, travel, entry, residence, *and settlement* of migrants and as far as possible for the members of their families. Such measures shall include the provision of an interpretation service, where necessary.

ARTICLE 4. VALIDITY OF DOCUMENTS

1. The parties shall determine the conditions to be met for purposes of recognition in the territory of immigration of any document issued by the competent authority of the territory of emigration in respect of migrants *and members of their families* [or in the case of refugees and displaced persons, by any body established in accordance with the terms of an international instrument which may be responsible for the protection of refugees and displaced persons who do not benefit from the protection of any Government] concerning—

(a) civil status ;
(b) legal status ;
(c) occupational qualifications ;
(d) general education and vocational training ; and
(e) participation in social security systems.

2. The parties shall also determine the application of such recognition.

[3. In the case of refugees and displaced persons, the competent authority of the territory of immigration shall recognise the validity of any travel document issued in lieu of a national passport by the competent authority of the territory of emigration and, in particular, of travel documents issued in accordance with the terms of an international Agreement (*e.g.,* the travel document established by the Agreement of 15 October 1946, and the Nansen passport).]

ARTICLE 5. CONDITIONS AND CRITERIA OF MIGRATION

1. The parties shall jointly determine—

(a) the requirements for migrants *and members of their families*, as to age, physical aptitude and health, as well as the occupational qualifications for the various branches

of economic activity and for the various occupational categories ;

(b) *the categories of the members of the migrants' families authorised to accompany or to join them.*

2.   The parties shall also determine, in accordance with the provisions of Article 28 of this Agreement:—

(a)   the numbers and occupational categories of migrants to be recruited in the course of a stated period ;

(b)   the areas of recruitment and the areas of placing and settlement [except that in the case of refugees and displaced persons the determination of the areas of recruitment shall be reserved to any body established in accordance with the terms of an international instrument which may be responsible for the protection of refugees and displaced persons who do not benefit from the protection of any Government].

3.   In order to recruit migrants required to meet the technical needs of the territory of immigration and who can adapt themselves easily to the conditions in the territory of immigration, the parties shall determine criteria to govern technical selection of the migrants.

4.   In drawing up these criteria, the two parties shall take into consideration—

(a)   with respect to medical selection :

   (i)   the nature of the medical examination which migrants shall undergo (general medical examination, X-ray examination, laboratory examination, etc.) ;

   (ii)   the drawing up of lists of diseases and physical defects which clearly constitute a disability for employment in certain occupations ;

   (iii)   minimum health provisions prescribed by international health conventions and relating to movement of population from one country to another ;

(b)   with respect to vocational selection :

   (i)   qualifications required of migrants with respect to each occupation or groups of occupations ;

   (ii)   enumeration of alternative occupations requiring similar qualifications or capacities on the part of the workers in order to fulfil the needs of specified occupations for which it is difficult to recruit a sufficient number of qualified workers ;

   (iii)   development of psycho-technical testing ;

(c)   with respect to selection based on the age of migrants, flexibility to be given to the application of age criteria in order to take into consideration on the one hand the requirements of various occupations and, on the other, the varying capacities of different individuals at a given age.

Article 6. Organisation of Recruitment, Introduction and Placing

1. The bodies or persons which engage in the operations of recruitment, introduction and placing of migrants *and of members of their families* shall be named by the competent authorities of the respective territories [or in the case of refugees and displaced persons, by any body established in accordance with the terms of an international instrument which may be responsible for the protection of refugees and displaced persons who do not benefit from the protection of any Government on the one hand and the competent authority of the territory of immigration on the other] subject to the approval of both parties.

2. Subject to the provisions of the following paragraphs, the right to engage in the operations of recruitment, introduction and placing shall be restricted to—

(a) public employment offices or other public bodies of the territory in which the operations take place ;

(b) public bodies of a territory other than that in which the operations take place which are authorised to operate in that territory by an agreement between the parties ;

(c) any body established in accordance with the terms of an international instrument.

3. In addition, in so far as the national laws and regulations of the parties permit and subject to the approval and supervision of the competent authorities of the parties, the operations of recruitment, introduction and placing may be undertaken by—

(a) the prospective employer or a person in his service acting on his behalf ; and

(b) private agencies.

4. The administrative costs of recruitment, introduction and placing shall not be borne by the migrants.

Article 7. Selection Testing

1. An intending migrant shall undergo an appropriate examination in the territory of emigration ; any such examination should inconvenience him as little as possible.

2. With respect to the organisation of the selection of migrants, the parties shall agree on—

(a) recognition and composition of official agencies or private bodies authorised by the competent authority of the territory of immigration to carry out selection operations in the territory of emigration ;

(b) organisation of selection examinations, the centres where they are to be carried out, and allocation of expenses resulting from these examinations ;

(c) co-operation of the competent authorities of the two parties and in particular of their employment services in organising selection.

ARTICLE 8. INFORMATION AND ASSISTANCE OF MIGRANTS

1. The migrant accepted after medical and occupational examination in the assembly or selection centre shall receive, in a language that he understands, all information he may still require as to the nature of the work for which he has been engaged, the region of employment, the undertaking to which he is assigned, travel arrangements and the conditions of life and work including health and related matters in the country and region to which he is going.

2. On arrival in the country of destination, and at a reception centre if such exists, or at the place of residence, migrants *and the members of their families* shall receive all the documents which they need for their work, their residence *and their settlement* in the country, as well as information, instruction and advice regarding conditions of life and work, and any other assistance that they may need to adapt themselves to the conditions in the country of immigration.

ARTICLE 9. EDUCATION AND VOCATIONAL TRAINING

The parties shall co-ordinate their activities concerning the organisation of educational courses for migrants, which shall include general information on the country of immigration, instruction in the language of that country, and vocational training.

ARTICLE 10. EXCHANGE OF TRAINEES

The parties agree to further the exchange of trainees, and to determine in a separate agreement the conditions governing such exchanges.

ARTICLE 11. CONDITIONS OF TRANSPORT

1. During the journey from their place of residence to the assembly or selection centre, as well as during their stay in the said centre, migrants *and the members of their families* shall receive from the competent authority of the territory of emigration [or in the case of refugees and displaced persons, from any body established in accordance with the terms of an international instrument which may be responsible for the protection of refugees and displaced persons who do not benefit from the protection of any Government] any assistance which they may require.

2. The competent authorities of the territories of emigration and immigration shall, each within its own jurisdiction, safe-

guard the health and welfare of, and render assistance to, migrants *and the members of their families* during the journey from the assembly or selection centre to the place of their employment, as well as during their stay in a reception centre if such exists.

3.   Migrants *and members of their families* shall be transported in a manner appropriate for human beings and in conformity with the laws and regulations in force.

4.   The parties shall agree upon the terms and conditions for the application of the provisions of this Article.

ARTICLE 12. TRAVEL AND MAINTENANCE EXPENSES

The parties shall agree upon the methods for meeting the cost of travel of the migrants *and the members of their families* from the place of their residence to the place of their destination, and the cost of their maintenance while travelling, sick or hospitalised, as well as the cost of transport of their personal belongings.

ARTICLE 13. TRANSFER OF FUNDS

1.   The competent authority of the territory of emigration shall, as far as possible and in conformity with national laws and regulations concerning the import and export of foreign currency, authorise and provide facilities for migrants *and for members of their families* to withdraw from their country such sums as they may need for their initial settlement abroad.

2.   The competent authority of the territory of immigration shall, as far as possible and in conformity with national laws and regulations concerning the import and export of foreign currency, authorise and provide facilities for the periodical transfer to the territory of emigration of migrants' savings and of any other sums due in virtue of this Agreement.

3.   The transfers of funds mentioned in paragraphs 1 and 2 above shall be made at the prevailing official rate of exchange.

4.   The parties shall take all measures necessary for the simplification and acceleration of administrative formalities regarding the transfer of funds so that such funds may be available with the least possible delay to those entitled to them.

5.   The parties shall determine if and under what conditions a migrant may be required to remit part of his wages for the maintenance of his family remaining in his country or in the territory from which he emigrated.

ARTICLE 14. ADAPTATION AND NATURALISATION

The competent authority of the territory of immigration shall take measures to facilitate adaptation to national climatic, economic and social conditions and facilitate the procedure of naturalisation of migrants and of members of their families.

ARTICLE 15. SUPERVISION OF LIVING AND WORKING
CONDITIONS

1. Provision shall be made for the supervision by the competent authority or duly authorised bodies of the territory of immigration of the living and working conditions, including hygienic conditions, to which the migrants are subject.

2. With respect to temporary migrants, the parties shall provide, where appropriate, for authorised representatives of the territory of emigration [or in the case of refugees and displaced persons, of any body established in accordance with the terms of an international instrument which may be responsible for the protection of refugees and displaced persons who do not benefit from the protection of any Government] to co-operate with the competent authority or duly authorised bodies of the territory of immigration in carrying out this supervision.

3. During a fixed period, the duration of which shall be determined by the parties, migrants shall receive special assistance in regard to matters concerning their conditions of employment.

4. Assistance with respect to the employment and living conditions of the migrants may be given either through the regular labour inspection service of the territory of immigration or through a special service for migrants, in co-operation where appropriate with approved voluntary organisations.

5. Provision shall be made where appropriate for the co-operation of representatives of the territory of emigration [or in the case of refugees and displaced persons, of any body established in accordance with the terms of an international instrument which may be responsible for the protection of refugees and displaced persons who do not benefit from the protection of any Government] with such services.

ARTICLE 16. SETTLEMENT OF DISPUTES

1. In case of a dispute between a migrant and his employer, the migrant shall have access to the appropriate courts or shall otherwise obtain redress for his grievances, in accordance with the laws and regulations of the territory of immigration.

2. The authorities shall establish such other machinery as is necessary to settle disputes arising out of the Agreement.

ARTICLE 17. EQUALITY OF TREATMENT

1. The competent authority of the territory of immigration shall grant to migrants *and to members of their families* with respect to employment in which they are eligible to engage treatment no less favourable than that applicable to its own nationals in virtue of legal or administrative provisions or collective labour agreements.

2. Such equality of treatment shall apply, without discrimination in respect of nationality, race, religion or sex, to immigrants lawfully within the territory of immigration in respect of the following matters :

(a) in so far as such matters are regulated by laws or regulations or are subject to the control of administrative authorities,

    (i) remuneration, including family allowances where these form part of remuneration, hours of work, weekly rest days, overtime arrangements, holidays with pay and other regulations concerning employment, including limitations on home work, minimum age provisions, women's work, and the work of young persons ;

    (ii) membership of trade unions and enjoyment of the benefits of collective bargaining ;

    (iii) admission to schools, to apprenticeship and to courses or schools for vocational or technical training, provided that this does not prejudice nationals of the country of immigration ;

    (iv) recreation and welfare measures ;

(b) employment taxes, dues or contributions payable in respect of the persons employed ;

(c) hygiene, safety and medical assistance ;

(d) legal proceedings relating to the matters referred to in this Agreement.

ARTICLE 18. ACCESS TO TRADES AND OCCUPATIONS AND THE RIGHT TO ACQUIRE PROPERTY

Equality of treatment shall also apply to—

(a) *access to trades and occupations to the extent permitted under national laws and regulations ;*

(b) *acquisition, possession and transmission of urban or rural property.*

ARTICLE 19. SUPPLY OF FOOD

The treatment applied to migrants *and the members of their families* shall be the same as that applied to national workers in the same occupation as regards the supply of food.

ARTICLE 20. HOUSING CONDITIONS

The competent authority of the territory of immigration shall ensure that migrants *and the members of their families* have hygienic and suitable housing, in so far as the necessary housing is available.

ARTICLE 21. SOCIAL SECURITY

1. The two parties shall determine in a separate agreement the methods of applying a system of social security to migrants and their dependants.

2. *Such agreement shall provide that the competent authority of the territory of immigration shall take measures to ensure to the migrants and their dependants treatment not less favourable than that afforded by it to its nationals, except where particular residence qualifications apply to nationals.*

3. *The agreement shall embody appropriate arrangements for the maintenance of migrants' acquired rights and rights in course of acquisition framed with due regard to the principles of the Maintenance of Migrants' Pension Rights Convention, 1935, or of any revision of that Convention.*

4. The agreement shall provide that the competent authority of the territory of immigration shall take measures to grant to temporary migrants and their dependants treatment not less favourable than that afforded by it to its nationals, subject in the case of compulsory pension schemes to appropriate arrangements being made for the maintenance of migrants' acquired rights and rights in course of acquisition.

ARTICLE 22. CONTRACTS OF EMPLOYMENT

1. In countries where a system of model contracts is used, the individual contract of employment for migrants shall be based on a model contract drawn up by the parties for the principal branches of economic activity.

2. The individual contract of employment shall set forth the general conditions of engagement and of employment provided in the relevant model contract and shall be translated into a language which the migrant understands. A copy of the contract shall be delivered to the migrant before departure from the territory of emigration or, if it is agreed between the two parties concerned, in a reception centre on arrival in the territory of immigration. In the latter case before departure the migrant shall be informed in writing by a document which relates either to him individually or to a group of migrants of which he is a member, of the occupational category in which he is to be engaged and the other conditions of work, in particular the minimum wage which is guaranteed to him.

3. The individual contract of employment shall contain necessary information, such as—

(a) the full name of the worker as well as the date and place of birth, his family status, his place of residence and of recruitment ;

(b) the nature of the work, and the place where it is to be performed ;

(c)   the occupational category in which he is placed ;

(d)   remuneration for ordinary hours of work, overtime, night work and holidays, and the medium for wage payment ;

(e)   bonuses, indemnities and allowances, if any ;

(f)   conditions under which and extent to which the employer may be authorised to make any deductions from remuneration ;

(g)   conditions regarding food if food is to be provided by the employer ;

(h)   the duration of the contract as well as the conditions of renewal and denunciation of the contract ;

(i)   the conditions under which entry and residence in the territory of immigration are permitted ;

(j)   the method of meeting the expenses of the journey of the migrant *and the members of his family* ;

(k)   in case of temporary migration, the method of meeting the expenses of return to the home country or the territory of migration, as appropriate ;

(l)   the grounds on which a contract may be prematurely terminated.

ARTICLE 23. CHANGE OF EMPLOYMENT

1.   If the competent authority of the territory of immigration considers that the employment for which the migrant has been recruited does not correspond to his physical capacity or occupational qualifications, the said authority shall provide facilities for placing the said migrant in an employment corresponding to his capacity or qualifications, and in which he may be employed in accordance with national laws or regulations.

2.   During periods of unemployment, if any, the method of maintaining the migrant *and the dependent members of his family authorised to accompany or join him* shall be determined by arrangements made under a separate agreement.

ARTICLE 24. EMPLOYMENT STABILITY

1.   If before the expiration of the period of his contract the migrant for employment becomes redundant in the undertaking or branch of economic activity for which he was engaged, the competent authority of the territory of immigration shall, subject to the provisions of the contract, facilitate the placing of the said migrant in other suitable employment in which he may be employed in accordance with national laws or regulations.

2.   If the migrant is not entitled to benefits under an unemployment insurance or assistance scheme, his maintenance, *as well as that of dependent members of his family,* during any

period in which he is unemployed shall be determined by a separate agreement in so far as this is not inconsistent with the terms of his contract.

3. The provisions of this Article shall not affect the right of the migrant to benefit from any provisions that may be included in his contract in case it is prematurely terminated by the employer.

ARTICLE 25. PROVISIONS CONCERNING COMPULSORY RETURN

1. The competent authority of the territory of immigration undertakes that a migrant *and the members of his family who have been authorised to accompany or join him* will not be returned to the territory from which he emigrated unless he so desires if, because of illness or injury, he is unable to follow his occupation.

2. The Government of the territory of immigration undertakes not to send refugees and displaced persons or migrants who do not wish to return to their country of origin for political reasons back to their territory of origin as distinct from the territory from which they were recruited, unless they formally express this desire by a request in writing addressed both to the competent authority of the territory of immigration and the representative of the body set up in accordance with the provisions of an international instrument which may be responsible for the protection of refugees and displaced persons who do not benefit from the protection of any Government.

ARTICLE 26. RETURN JOURNEY

1. The cost of the return journey of a migrant introduced under a plan sponsored by the Government of the territory of immigration, who is obliged to leave his employment for reasons for which he is not responsible, and who cannot, in virtue of national laws and regulations, be placed in an employment for which he is eligible, shall be regulated as follows :

(a) the cost of the return journey of the migrant, and persons dependent upon him, shall in no case fall on the migrant himself ;

(b) supplementary bilateral agreements shall specify the method of meeting the cost of this return journey ;

(c) in any case, even if no provision to this effect is included in a bilateral agreement, the information given to migrants at the time of their recruitment shall specify what person or agency is responsible for defraying the cost of return in the circumstances mentioned in this Article.

2. In accordance with the methods of co-operation and consultation agreed upon under Article 28 of this Agreement, the two parties shall determine the measures necessary to organ-

ise the return home of the said persons and to assure to them in the course of the journey the conditions of health and welfare and the assistance which they enjoyed during the outward journey.

3.   The competent authority of the territory of emigration shall exempt from customs duties on their arrival—

(a)   personal effects ; and

(b)   portable hand-tools and portable equipment of the kind normally owned by workers for the carrying out of their particular trades, which have been in possession and use of the said persons for an appreciable time and which are intended to be used by them in the course of their occupation.

ARTICLE 27. DOUBLE TAXATION

The two parties shall determine in a separate agreement the measures to be taken to avoid double taxation on the earnings of a migrant for employment.

ARTICLE 28. METHODS OF CO-OPERATION

1.   The two parties shall agree on the methods of consultation and co-operation necessary to carry out the terms of the Agreement.

2.   When so requested by the representatives of the two parties the International Labour Office shall be associated with such consultation and co-operation.

ARTICLE 29. FINAL PROVISIONS

1.   The parties shall determine the duration of the Agreement as well as the period of notice for termination.

2.   The parties shall determine those provisions of this Agreement which shall remain in operation after expiration of this Agreement.

Recommendation 151
_____

RECOMMENDATION CONCERNING MIGRANT WORKERS.

The General Conference of the International Labour Organisation,

Having been convened at Geneva by the Governing Body of the International Labour Office, and having met in its Sixtieth Session on 4 June 1975, and

Considering that the Preamble of the Constitution of the International Labour Organisation assigns to it the task of protecting " the interests of workers when employed in countries other than their own ", and

Recalling the provisions contained in the Migration for Employment Convention and Recommendation (Revised), 1949, and in the Protection of Migrant Workers (Underdeveloped Countries) Recommendation, 1955, which deal with such matters as the preparation and organisation of migration, social services to be provided to migrant workers and their families, in particular before their departure and during their journey, equality of treatment as regards a variety of matters which they enumerate, and the regulation of the stay and return of migrant workers and their families, and

Having adopted the Migrant Workers (Supplementary Provisions) Convention, 1975, and

Considering that further standards are desirable as regards equality of opportunity and treatment, social policy in regard to migrants and employment and residence, and

Having decided upon the adoption of certain proposals with regard to migrant workers, which is the fifth item on the agenda of the session, and

Having determined that these proposals shall take the form of a Recommendation, adopts this twenty-fourth day of June of the year one thousand nine hundred and seventy-five the following Recommendation, which may be cited as the Migrant Workers Recommendation, 1975:

1. Members should apply the provisions of this Recommendation within the framework of a coherent policy on international migration for employment. That policy should be based upon the economic and social needs of both countries of origin and countries of employment; it should take account not only of short-term manpower needs and resources but also of the long-term social and economic consequences of migration for migrants as well as for the communities concerned.

I. EQUALITY OF OPPORTUNITY AND TREATMENT

2. Migrant workers and members of their families lawfully within the territory of a Member should enjoy effective equality of opportunity and treatment with nationals of the Member concerned in respect of—

(a) access to vocational guidance and placement services;

(b) access to vocational training and employment of their own choice on the basis of individual suitability for such training or employment, account being taken

_____

ILO Instruments pertaining to Migrant Workers, *Convention 143* (1975). Reprinted with permission.

of qualifications acquired outside the territory of and in the country of employment;

(c) advancement in accordance with their individual character, experience, ability and diligence;

(d) security of employment, the provision of alternative employment, relief work and retraining;

(e) remuneration for work of equal value;

(f) conditions of work, including hours of work, rest periods, annual holidays with pay, occupational safety and occupational health measures, as well as social security measures and welfare facilities and benefits provided in connection with employment;

(g) membership of trade unions, exercise of trade union rights and eligibility for office in trade unions and in labour-management relations bodies, including bodies representing workers in undertakings;

(h) rights of full membership in any form of co-operative;

(i) conditions of life, including housing and the benefits of social services and educational and health facilities.

3. Each Member should ensure the application of the principles set forth in Paragraph 2 of this Recommendation in all activities under the control of a public authority and promote its observance in all other activities by methods appropriate to national conditions and practice.

4. Appropriate measures should be taken, with the collaboration of employers' and workers' organisations and other bodies concerned, with a view to—

(a) fostering public understanding and acceptance of the above-mentioned principles;

(b) examining complaints that these principles are not being observed and securing the correction, by conciliation or other appropriate means, of any practices regarded as in conflict therewith.

5. Each Member should ensure that national laws and regulations concerning residence in its territory are so applied that the lawful exercise of rights enjoyed in pursuance of these principles cannot be the reason for non-renewal of a residence permit or for expulsion and is not inhibited by the threat of such measures.

6. A Member may—

(a) make the free choice of employment, while assuring migrant workers the right to geographical mobility, subject to the conditions that the migrant worker has resided lawfully in its territory for the purpose of employment for a prescribed period not exceeding two years or, if its laws or regulations provide for contracts for a fixed term of less than two years, that the worker has completed his first work contract;

(b) after appropriate consultation with the representative organisations of employers and workers, make regulations concerning recognition of occupational qualifications acquired outside its territory, including certificates and diplomas;

(c) restrict access to limited categories of employment or functions where this is necessary in the interests of the State.

7. (1) In order to enable migrant workers and their families to take full advantage of their rights and opportunities in employment and occupation, such measures as may be necessary should be taken, in consultation with the representative organisations of employers and workers—

(a) to inform them, as far as possible in their mother tongue or, if that is not possible, in a language with which they are familiar, of their rights under national law and practice as regards the matters dealt with in Paragraph 2 of this Recommendation;

(b) to advance their knowledge of the language or languages of the country of employment, as far as possible during paid time;

(c) generally, to promote their adaptation to the society of the country of employment and to assist and encourage the efforts of migrant workers and their families to preserve their national and ethnic identity and their cultural ties with their country of origin, including the possibility for children to be given some knowledge of their mother tongue.

(2) Where agreements concerning the collective recruitment of workers have been concluded between Members, they should jointly take the necessary measures before the migrants' departure from their country of origin to introduce them to the language of the country of employment and also to its economic, social and cultural environment.

8. (1) Without prejudice to measures designed to ensure that migrant workers and their families enter national territory and are admitted to employment in conformity with the relevant laws and regulations, a decision should be taken as soon as possible in cases in which these laws and regulations have not been respected so that the migrant worker should know whether his position can be regularised or not.

(2) Migrant workers whose position has been regularised should benefit from all rights which, in accordance with Paragraph 2 of this Recommendation, are provided for migrant workers lawfully within the territory of a Member.

(3) Migrant workers whose position has not been or could not be regularised should enjoy equality of treatment for themselves and their families in respect of rights arising out of present and past employment as regards remuneration, social security and other benefits as well as regards trade union membership and exercise of trade union rights.

(4) In case of dispute about the rights referred to in the preceding subparagraphs, the worker should have the possibility of presenting his case to a competent body, either himself or through a representative.

(5) In case of expulsion of the worker or his family, the cost should not be borne by them.

II. Social Policy

9. Each Member should, in consultation with representative organisations of employers and workers, formulate and apply a social policy appropriate to national conditions and practice which enables migrant workers and their families to share in advantages enjoyed by its nationals while taking account, without adversely affecting the principle of equality of opportunity and treatment, of such special needs as they may have until they are adapted to the society of the country of employment.

10. With a view to making the policy as responsive as possible to the real needs of migrant workers and their families, it should be based, in particular, on an examination not only of conditions in the territory of the Member but also of those in the countries of origin of the migrants.

11. The policy should take account of the need to spread the social cost of migration as widely and equitably as possible over the entire collectivity of the country of employment, and in particular over those who profit most from the work of migrants.

12. The policy should be periodically reviewed and evaluated and where necessary revised.

A. *Reunification of Families*

13. (1) All possible measures should be taken both by countries of employment and by countries of origin to facilitate the reunification of families of migrant workers as rapidly as possible. These measures should include, as necessary, national laws or regulations and bilateral and multilateral arrangements.

(2) A prerequisite for the reunification of families should be that the worker has, for his family, appropriate accommodation which meets the standards normally applicable to nationals of the country of employment.

14. Representatives of all concerned, and in particular of employers and workers, should be consulted on the measures to be adopted to facilitate the reunification of families and their co-operation sought in giving effect thereto.

15. For the purpose of the provisions of this Recommendation relating to the reunification of families, the family of the migrant worker should include the spouse and dependent children, father and mother.

16. With a view to facilitating the reunification of families as quickly as possible in accordance with Paragraph 13 of this Recommendation, each Member should take full account of the needs of migrant workers and their families in particular in its policy regarding the construction of family housing, assistance in obtaining this housing and the development of appropriate reception services.

17. Where a migrant worker who has been employed for at least one year in a country of employment cannot be joined by his family in that country, he should be entitled—

(a) to visit the country of residence of his family during the paid annual holiday to which he is entitled under the national law and practice of the country of employment without losing during the absence from that country any acquired rights or rights in course of acquisition and, particularly, without having his employment terminated or his right to residence in the country of employment withdrawn during that period; or

(b) to be visited by his family for a period corresponding at least to the annual holiday with pay to which he is entitled.

18. Consideration should be given to the possibility of giving the migrant worker financial assistance towards the cost of the travel envisaged in the preceding Paragraph or a reduction in the normal cost of transport, for instance by the arrangement of group travel.

19. Without prejudice to more favourable provisions which may be applicable to them, persons admitted in pursuance of international arrangements for free movement of labour should have the benefit of the measures provided for in Paragraphs 13 to 18 of this Recommendation.

B. *Protection of the Health of Migrant Workers*

20. All appropriate measures should be taken to prevent any special health risks to which migrant workers may be exposed.

21. (1) Every effort should be made to ensure that migrant workers receive training and instruction in occupational safety and occupational hygiene in con-

nection with their practical training or other work preparation and, as far as possible, as part thereof.

(2) In addition, a migrant worker should, during paid working hours and immediately after beginning his employment, be provided with sufficient information in his mother tongue or, if that is not possible, in a language with which he is familiar, on the essential elements of laws and regulations and on provisions of collective agreements concerning the protection of workers and the prevention of accidents as well as on safety regulations and procedures particular to the nature of the work.

22. (1) Employers should take all possible measures so that migrant workers may fully understand instructions, warnings, symbols and other signs relating to safety and health hazards at work.

(2) Where, on account of the migrant workers' lack of familiarity with processes, language difficulties or other reasons, the training or instruction given to other workers is inadequate for them, special measures which ensure their full understanding should be taken.

(3) Members should have laws or regulations applying the principles set out in this Paragraph and provide that where employers or other persons or organisations having responsibility in this regard fail to observe such laws or regulations, administrative, civil and penal sanctions might be imposed.

C. *Social Services*

23. In accordance with the provisions of Paragraph 2 of this Recommendation, migrant workers and their families should benefit from the activities of social services and have access thereto under the same conditions as nationals of the country of employment.

24. In addition, social services should be provided which perform, in particular, the following functions in relation to migrant workers and their families—

(a) giving migrant workers and their families every assistance in adapting to the economic, social and cultural environment of the country of employment;

(b) helping migrant workers and their families to obtain information and advice from appropriate bodies, for instance by providing interpretation and translation services; to comply with administrative and other formalities; and to make full use of services and facilities provided in such fields as education, vocational training and language training, health services and social security, housing, transport and recreation: Provided that migrant workers and their families should as far as possible have the right to communicate with public authorities in the country of employment in their own language or in a language with which they are familiar, particularly in the context of legal assistance and court proceedings;

(c) assisting authorities and bodies with responsibilities relating to the conditions of life and work of migrant workers and their families in identifying their needs and in adapting thereto;

(d) giving the competent authorities information and, as appropriate, advice regarding the formulation, implementation and evaluation of social policy with respect to migrant workers;

(e) providing information for fellow workers and foremen and supervisors about the situation and the problems of migrant workers.

25. (1) The social services referred to in Paragraph 24 of this Recommendation may be provided, as appropriate to national conditions and practice, by public

authorities, by approved non-profit-making organisations or bodies, or by a combination of both. The public authorities should have the over-all responsibility of ensuring that these social services are at the disposal of migrant workers and their families.

(2) Full use should be made of services which are or can be provided by authorities, organisations and bodies serving the nationals of the country of employment, including employers' and workers' organisations.

26. Each Member should take such measures as may be necessary to ensure that sufficient resources and adequately trained staff are available for the social services referred to in Paragraph 24 of this Recommendation.

27. Each Member should promote co-operation and co-ordination between different social services on its territory and, as appropriate, between these services and corresponding services in other countries, without, however, this co-operation and co-ordination relieving the States of their responsibilities in this field.

28. Each Member should organise and encourage the organisation, at the national, regional or local level, or as appropriate in a branch of economic activity employing substantial numbers of migrant workers, of periodic meetings for the exchange of information and experience. Consideration should also be given to the exchange of information and experience with other countries of employment as well as with the countries of origin of migrant workers.

29. Representatives of all concerned and in particular of employers and workers should be consulted on the organisation of the social services in question and their co-operation sought in achieving the purposes aimed at.

III. EMPLOYMENT AND RESIDENCE

30. In pursuance of the provision of Paragraph 18 of the Migration for Employment Recommendation (Revised), 1949, that Members should, as far as possible, refrain from removing from their territory, on account of lack of means or the state of the employment market, a migrant worker regularly admitted thereto, the loss by such migrant worker of his employment should not in itself imply the withdrawal of his authorisation of residence.

31. A migrant who has lost his employment should be allowed sufficient time to find alternative employment, at least for a period corresponding to that during which he may be entitled to unemployment benefit; the authorisation of residence should be extended accordingly.

32. (1) A migrant worker who has lodged an appeal against the termination of his employment, under such procedures as may be available, should be allowed sufficient time to obtain a final decision thereon.

(2) If it is established that the termination of employment was not justified, the migrant worker should be entitled, on the same terms as national workers, to reinstatement, to compensation for loss of wages or of other payment which results from unjustified termination, or to access to a new job with a right to indemnification. If he is not reinstated, he should be allowed sufficient time to find alternative employment.

33. A migrant worker who is the object of an expulsion order should have a right of appeal before an administrative or judicial instance, according to conditions laid down in national laws or regulations. This appeal should stay the execution of the expulsion order, subject to the duly substantiated requirements of national security

or public order. The migrant worker should have the same right to legal assistance as national workers and have the possibility of being assisted by an interpreter.

34. (1) A migrant worker who leaves the country of employment should be entitled, irrespective of the legality of his stay therein—

(a) to any outstanding remuneration for work performed, including severance payments normally due;

(b) to benefits which may be due in respect of any employment injury suffered;

(c) in accordance with national practice—

    (i) to compensation in lieu of any holiday entitlement acquired but not used;

    (ii) to reimbursement of any social security contributions which have not given and will not give rise to rights under national laws or regulations or inter-national arrangements: Provided that where social security contributions do not permit entitlement to benefits, every effort should be made with a view to the conclusion of bilateral or multilateral agreements to protect the rights of migrants.

(2) Where any claim covered in subparagraph (1) of this Paragraph is in dispute, the worker should be able to have his interests represented before the competent body and enjoy equal treatment with national workers as regards legal assistance.

Appendix C:
Ratification Chart
of ILO Conventions
concerning Migrant
Workers

Appendix C

Convention	Federal Republic of Germany	France	Switzerland	United States
2 (Unemployment (1919)	Yes	Yes	Yes	No
19 (Equality of treatment (1925)	Yes	Yes	Yes	No
48 (1935)	No	No	No	No
97 (Migrant workers) (1949)	Yes	Yes[a]	No	No
118 (1962)	Yes[b]	Yes[c]	No	No
143 (Migrant workers) (1975)	No	No	No	No

Source: ILO, chart of Ratifications of International Labour Conventions (January 1, 1980).
[a]Excluding annex II.
[b]Excluding branches A,B,C,G, and H.
[c]Excluding A,B,C,D,F,G, and I.

Appendix D:
Council of Europe
Convention
Ratifications

Appendix D

Convention	Signed	France	Switzerland	Federal Republic of Germany
European Convention for the Protection of Human Rights and Fundamental Freedoms	1950	1974	1974	1952
Protocols				
1	1952	1974	1976	1957
2	1963	—	1974	1969
3	1963	1974	1974	1969
4	1963	1974	—	1968
5	1966	1974	1974	1969
European Convention on Establishment	1955	—	—	1965
European Social Charter	1961	1973	"1976"	1965
European Code of Social Security	1964	"1976"	1977	1971
Protocol to the European Code of Social Security	1964	"1976"	—	1971
Convention on the Legal Status of Migrant Workers	1977	—	—	—

Note: Quotation marks indicate signed but not ratified.

Appendix E: Development of the European Economic Community

1957 Treaty of Rome signatories and founding members: Italy, France, the Federal Republic of Germany, Belgium, the Netherlands, and Luxembourg.

1967 Merger of the EEC, the European Coal and Steel Community (ECSC) and the Eurotom Commission into a single institution whose governing body, the Commission, superseded the High Authority of the ECSC, the EEC, and the Euratom Councils.

1972 Treaty of Accession and "Europe of 9": Denmark, the United Kingdom, and Ireland join.

1981 "Europe of 10": Greece officially joins but free-labor movement will not apply to Greeks until 1988.

Spain and Portugal are EEC associate members that have formally applied for full membership. There have been unofficial talks concerning Turkish entry, but the prospect of full Turkish membership appears dim, while Spain and Portugal will likely become full members by 1985. Associate membership confers preferential treatment by EEC members in economic affairs. For example, if labor recruitment were to begin anew, workers from Spain, Portugal, and Turkey would be given preference over other non-EEC workers. Associate status also extends to the realm of foreign policy. The needs of associates will be given special considerations by EEC members. In Western Europe, the term *European Community* has largely supplanted usage of EEC or Common Market when referring to the supranational institutions stemming from the Treaty of Rome.

Appendix F:
Franco-African Treaties concerning Migrant Workers

Appendix F

	Establishment Conventions			Circulation Conventions		
	Multilateral Accord of 1960	Bilateral Treaty Similar to 1960 Accords	Bilateral Treaties on the 1974 Model	1963-Type Circulation Treaty	1974 Model Treaty	Other
Benin	—	—	—	1971	1975[a]	—
Cameroon	1960	—	—	—	1976	Free circulation
Central African Republic	1960	1960	1974[a]	—	—	Free circulation
Congo	—	1960	—	1970	1974[a]	—
Ivory Coast	1960	—	—	1974	1976[a]	—
Gabon	1960	1960	1974[a]	1970	Being negotiated	—
Upper Volta	—	—	—	—	—	Common law
Madagascar	—	—	1977[a]	1963	1977[a]	—
Mali	—	—	—	1963	Being negotiated	—
Mauritania	—	—	—	1970	1977[a]	—
Niger	—	—	1974	—	1974	—
Senegal	1961	1960	—	—	—	Free circulation
Chad	—	1963	—	—	—	—
Togo	—	—	—	1970	1976[a]	—

Source: Jacques Picard, ''Les conventions bilaterales passés par la France,'' *Les travailleurs étrangers et le droit international*, ed. Société Française pour le droit international (Paris: Editions A. Pedone, 1979), p. 115. Reprinted with permission.

[a]Treaty is not in effect.

Appendix G: Summary of Accords on Labor Signed by France with Main Labor-Supplying Countries

Appendix G

Country	Date of Accord	Recruitment				Families			Status				Professional Training	
		Contract	Contingent	Age Limit	Medical Test	Allowed	Privileged Entry	Subject to Adequate Housing	Carte de Travail	Carte de Sejour	Subject to Fontanet Circular	Can Have Another Job	Access Granted	Separate Agreement
Algeria	4/64	No	Yes[a]	No	Yes	Yes		Yes	No	No	No	Yes	Yes	No
	12/68	No	Yes[b]	No	Yes	Yes		Yes	No	Yes		Yes	Yes	No
Portugal	12/63	Yes	No	Yes	Yes	Not included	Yes[d]		Yes	Yes		[e]	Yes	Yes
	7/71	Yes	Yes[c]	Yes	Yes		Yes[d]		Yes	Yes		[e]	Yes	–
Spain	1/61	Yes	No	Yes	Yes	Yes		Yes	Yes	Yes	Yes	[e]	Yes	No
Tunisia	8/63	Yes	No	Yes	Yes	Yes		Yes	Yes	Yes	Yes	[e]	Yes	Yes
Morocco	6/63	Yes	No	Yes	Yes	Yes		Yes	Yes	Yes	Yes	[e]	Not included	Yes
Turkey	4/65	Yes	No	No	Yes	Yes		Yes	Yes	Yes	Yes		Yes	Yes
Yugoslavia	1/65	Yes	No	Yes	Yes	Yes		Yes	Yes	Yes	Yes	Yes	Yes	Yes[d]

Source: Adapted from Stephen Adler, *International Migration and Dependence*, (Hempstead, England: Saxon House, 1977), p. 96.

[a] Contingent fixed by France.

[b] Fixed for three years at 35,000, then for two years at 25,000.

[c] Maximum 65,000 per year.

[d] Separate annex to accord.

[e] May be allowed after first year.

[f] The Fontanet circular sought to curb legalization of illegal aliens.

Appendix H: Summary of International Instruments and Guidelines pertaining to European Foreign-Worker Policy

Labor Mobility

EEC Regulation 1612/68 (1968), §1: "Every national of a Member State, whatever his place of residence, has the right of access to salaried activity and to exercise this right on the territory of another Member State, in accordance with the legal, statutory and administrative dispositions regulating the employment of national workers of that State."

Draft European Convention on the Legal Status of Migrant Workers (1971), §4(1): "The Contracting Parties concerned shall guarantee the following rights to migrant workers:—the right to leave (etc.)—the right to admission to the territory of a Contracting Party in order to take up paid employment, after having been authorized to do so and after obtaining the necessary papers."

Information Services

European Social Charter (1965), §19(1): "The Contracting Parties undertake: (1) to maintain or to satisfy themselves that there are maintained adequate and free services to assist such workers, particularly in obtaining accurate information, and take all appropriate steps, so far as national laws and regulations permit, against misleading propaganda relating to emigration and immigration."

Final Act of the Helsinki Conference on Security and Cooperation in Europe (1 August 1975): "Economic and Social Aspects of Migrant Labour: . . . to confirm the right of migrant workers to receive as far as possible, regular information in their own language, covering both their country of origin and the host country."

Adapted from International Catholic Migration Commission, *Principles and Guidelines for the Elaboration of a Statute for Migrants* (Geneva, 1976).

Counseling and Specialized Social Assistance

European Social Charter (1965), §19: "The Contracting Parties undertake . . . (2) to adopt appropriate measures within their own jurisdiction to facilitate the departure, journey and reception of such workers and their families."

Draft European Convention on the Legal Status of Migrant Workers (1971) §10(2): "For this reception, migrant workers and members of their families shall be entitled, in the same way as national workers, to assistance from the employment services or the social services. . . . Each Contracting Party shall endeavor to ensure that special social services are available, whenever the situation so demands, to facilitate or coordinate the reception of migrant workers and their families."

Recommendation 712 of the Consultative Assembly of the Council of Europe (1975): "The Assembly recommends . . . in the social and economic fields: (1) Establishment of information and advice centers . . . so as to enable foreign workers to settle in more easily and familiarize themselves more quickly with their living and working environment."

Employer Sanctions

Council of Europe Recommendation 712 of Its Consultative Assembly (1973), (d) 9: "Intensification of investigations concerning the employment of illegal immigrants with fines or prison sentences for offending employers and persons responsible for organizing the clandestine entry of such persons into immigration countries."

Council of Europe Resolution (74)14 of Its Committee of Ministers (May 1974): "Invites Governments to . . . (d) take care to prevent by the appropriate means the introduction of clandestine foreign manpower and its exploitation, in particular by taking effective sanctions against those responsible for these abuses."

Right to Work

Resolution (74)15 of the Committee of Ministers of the Council of Europe (1974): "The Committee of Ministers recommends the Governments of Member States to take, where necessary, measures in the fields enumerated below. . . . Foresee, on the immigration of every migrant worker, the conclusion of a work contract of a length sufficient to enable him to clearly appreciate his situation before the end of employment and to effect a responsible choice for the future.''

Final Act of the Helsinki Conference on Security and Cooperation in Europe (1 August 1975): "Economic and social aspects of migrant labor: . . . to endeavor to ensure, as far as possible, that migrant workers may enjoy the same opportunities as nationals of the host country of finding other suitable employment in the event of unemployment.''

Employment and Social Rights

Draft European Convention on the Legal Status of Migrant Workers (19) §20: "With regard to the prevention of industrial accidents and occupational diseases and to industrial hygiene, migrant workers shall enjoy the same rights and protection as national workers, in application of national legislation and collective agreements.''

EEC Regulation 1612/68 Relative to Free Circulation (1968), §1(3): "The migrant worker also benefits, in the same way and in the same conditions as national workers, from the teaching in vocational training schools and readaptation or retraining centers.''

Draft European Convention on the Legal Status of Migrant Workers (1971) §14(1): "Migrant workers and members of their families, officially admitted to the territory of a Contracting Party, shall be entitled to the same basis and under the same conditions as national workers, to general education, apprenticeship and vocational training and occupational rehabilitation.''

Resolution 712 of the Consultative Assembly of the Council of Europe (1973), Annex §5: "Give migrant workers the same possibilities as national workers to complete their vocational training, especially the obtention of grants.''

Resolution (74)15 of the Committee of Ministers of the Council of Europe on the Equality of Treatment of National and Migrant Workers (1974), §5: "Vocational Readaptation: Enable the migrant workers to benefit in the same way as the national worker from the facilities for vocational readaptation offered by the competent bodies of the immigration country.'' §7: "Favor social and professional advancement as well as the migrant worker's integration within the enterprise.''

Family Rights

Universal Declaration of Human Rights (1948), §16(3): "The family is the natural and fundamental group unit of society and is entitled to protection by society and the State."

EEC Regulation 1612/68 on Free Circulation (1968), §10: "Entitled to settle with the worker coming from a Member State employed on the territory of another Member State, whatever their nationality, are: (a) his spouse and their descendants under 21 years of age or dependent on him, (b) ascendants of this worker and his spouse who are their dependents.

Resolution of the Advisory Committee of the Special Representative of the Council of Europe for Refugees and Overpopulation (May 1973): "The Committee of Ministers recommends to the Governments of Member States to be guided, as regards the reunion of migrant worker's families, by the following general principles: (1) the reunion of the migrant worker's family should, as far as possible, be recognized as a right, including in internal legislation."

Recommendation of the OECD Council on the Introduction and Employment of Foreign Manpower (30 September 1961), §2 (III): "The Council, on the proposal of the Manpower Committee, recommends the Governments of Member Countries take the following measures: (III) Measures in Favor of the Wives and Children of Foreign Workers: (a) that the permit or other residence authorizations, both when they are first granted or when they are renewed are the same kind and bear the same expiry date as the document held by the head of the family . . . (b) that the residence status of these persons be identical to that of the head of the family's in the shortest possible time."

European Social Charter (1965), §19(6): "The Contracting Parties undertake: (6) to facilitate as far as possible the reunion of the family of a foreign worker permitted to establish himself in the territory."

Final Act of the Helsinki Conference on Security and Cooperation in Europe (1 August 1975), "Economic and Social Aspects of Migrant Labour": "To facilitate, as far as possible, the reuniting of migrant workers with their families." Human Contacts: (b) "reunification of families: The participating States will deal in a positive and humanitarian spirit with the application of persons who wish to be reunited with members of their family, with special attention being given to requests of an urgent character, such as requests submitted by persons who are ill or old."

Housing

Recommendation 712 of the Consultative Assembly of the Council of Europe on the Integration of Migrant Workers (1973), Annex §4: "Authorize the family reunion of permanent migrant workers after 12 months and take adequate measures in order that this reunion be favored by putting at their disposal accommodation considered as normal in the regions where they are employed."

Resolution (74)14 of the Committee of Ministers of the Council of Europe (1974): "[The Committee of Ministers invites the Governments of Member States] . . . to solve the problem of housing, in order to enable family reunion through a program of international cooperation which also take into account the possibility of making a wider use of the Council's Resettlement Funds."

European Social Charter (1965), §19(4): "To secure for such working lawfully within their territories . . . treatment not less favorable than that of their own nationals in respect of the following matters (c) accommodation."

EEC Regulation 1612/68 (1968), §9(1): "The worker who is a national of a Member State . . . benefits from all those rights and advantages granted to national workers with regard to accommodation in those places where such lists are kept and he benefits from the advantages and priorities that follow from this."

Migrant Child Education

Draft European Convention on the Legal Status of Migrant Workers (19) §14(1): "Migrant workers and members of their families, officially admitted to the territory of a Contracting Party, shall be entitled on the same basis and under the same conditions as national workers, to general education, apprenticeship." §14(2): "To facilitate access to general and vocational schools . . . the Contracting Parties shall facilitate, where necessary, the teaching of the language(s) of the immigration country to migrant workers and members of their families." §14(3): "The application of this provision to the granting of scholarships shall be left to the discretion of each Contracting Party." §31(3): "To facilitate the possible return to their country of origin of migrant workers' children, referred to in Article XII, the interested Contracting Parties shall act by common accord to ensure that instruction is provided in the language of the migration country."

Final Act of the Helsinki Conference on Security and Cooperation in Europe (1 August 1975): "Economic and social aspects of migrant labor: . . . to ensure that the children of migrant workers established in the host country have access to the education usually given there, under the same conditions as the children of that country, and, furthermore, to permit them to receive supplementary education in their own language on national culture, history and geography."

Social Security and Family Allowances

Universal Declaration of Human Rights (1948), §22: "Everyone, as a member of society, has the right to social security."

Draft European Convention on the Legal Status of Migrant Workers (1971), §18(1): "Each Contracting Party undertakes to grant, with its territory, to migrant workers and members of their families, equity of treatment with its own nationals, in the matter of social security, subject to conditions required by national legislation and by lateral or multilateral agreements already concluded or to be concluded between the Parties concerned." §18(2): "The Contracting Parties shall moreover endeavor to secure to migrant workers and members of their families the conservation of the rights in course of acquisition and acquired rights, as well as provision of benefits abroad, through bilateral and multilateral agreements."

Trade Union Rights

ILO Recommendation 100 (1951), §41: "It would be fitting to recognize migrant workers' right to association and right to freely involve themselves in all union activities that are not contrary to the laws in the centers where they work, and all possible measures should be taken to ensure union organizations representing the interested workers the right to conclude collective conventions with employers and with employer organizations."

European Social Charter (1965), §19(4): "The Contracting Parties undertake . . . to secure for migrant workers . . . (b) membership of trade unions and enjoyment of the benefit of collective bargaining."

U.N. Covenant on Economic, Social and Cultural Rights (1966), §8(1): "The States Parties to the present Covenant undertake to ensure (a) the right of everyone to form trade unions and join the trade union of his choice . . . (d) the right to strike, provided that it is exercised in conformity with the laws of the particular country."

EEC Regulation 1612/68 (1968) Concerning Free Circulation, §8: "The worker who is a citizen of a Member State and is occupied on the territory of another Member State, benefits from equality of treatment in the matter of affiliation to trade unions and the exercise of trade union rights, including the right to vote. . . . He benefits furthermore from the right of eligibility to the organs representing workers in an enterprise."

Draft European Convention on the Legal Status of Migrant Workers (1971), §28: "The Contracting Parties shall allow migrant workers the right to form and to join organizations for the protection of their economic and social interests, under the legal provisions operating in the immigration country and the measures taken in the matter by the social partners."

Legal Guarantees

European Social Charter (1965), §19(7): "The Contracting Parties undertake: (7) to secure for such workers lawfully within their territories treatment not less favorable than that of their own nationals in respect of legal proceedings relating to matters referred to in this Article."

Draft European Convention on the Legal Status of Migrant Workers (1971), §26(1): "The Contracting Parties undertake to secure to migrant workers treatment not less favorable than that of their own nationals in respect of legal proceedings." §26(2): "Each Contracting Party shall provide the migrant workers of the other Contracting Parties with legal aid on the same conditions as for their own nationals and, in the cases of civil or criminal proceedings, the possibility of obtaining the assistance of an interpreter where they cannot understand or speak the language used in Court."

Resolution (74)15 of the Committee of Ministers of the Council of Europe (1974), §11: "Right to appeal: guarantee to the migrant worker in the same conditions as the national worker, the exercise of the right of appeal to the competent bodies in the event of litigation relative to dismissal."

Permit Renewal

Recommendation 712 of the Consultative Assembly of the Council of Europe (1973): "The Assembly recommends that the Committee of Ministers invite the governments of immigration countries among Council of Europe Member States: . . . (d) granting to migrant workers, after five years' uninterrupted residence of a work and residence permit of unlimited duration which cannot be withdrawn, except in exceptional circumstances."

Draft European Convention on the Legal Status of Migrant Workers (1971), §25 (Re-employment): "(1) If a migrant worker loses his job for reasons beyond his control, such as redundancy or prolonged illness, the competent authority of the immigration country shall help him to find some other employment, subject to the laws and regulations of that country. (2) To this end the Contracting Party concerned shall, where possible, promote suitable measures for the occupational rehabilitation of the migrant worker in question, provided that he intends to continue in employment in the country concerned afterwards."

Resolution (74)15 of the Committee of Ministers of the Council of Europe (1974): "The Committee of Ministers . . . recommends to the Governments of Member States to take, if necessary, measures in the fields enumerated below. . . . *V.* Vocational Readaptation: To enable migrant workers to benefit, under the same powers as national workers, from the facilities of vocational readaptation offered by the competent organs of the immigration State. . . . *X.* Non-discrimination in the matter of dismissal: To avoid, through measures corresponding to the national situation, all discrimination between the migrant and national workers, in the field of dismissals."

**Appendix I:
Rights Accorded to
Various Categories of
Permit Holders**

Appendix I:

	Routine Renewal	Family Entry	Family Visiting Rights	Unemployment Insurance	Social Security Benefits (Accident, Health, Disability)	Access to Vocational Training and Social Services	Unionization Possibility
France							
Seasonal	No	No[a]	Yes	Yes	Yes	No	Yes
One year or "A permits"	No	No	Yes	Yes	Yes	Yes	Yes
"Ordinary or B" (1–10 years)	No	Yes	Yes	Yes	Yes	Yes	Yes
Privileged "C Permits"	Yes[b]	Yes	Yes	Yes	Yes	Yes	Yes
Switzerland							
Seasonal	No	No	Yes	No	Yes	No	Yes
First year	No	No[c]	Yes	Yes	Yes	Yes	Yes
Annuals (2–4 years)	No	Yes	Yes	Yes	Yes	Yes	Yes
Two-year-permits (5–10 years)	Yes	Yes	Yes	Yes	Yes	Yes	Yes
10 yr. + (C certificates)	Yes	Yes	Yes	Yes	Yes	Yes	Yes
Germany							
One year	No	No	Yes	Yes	Yes	No	Yes
2–5 years (general permits)	No	Yes	Yes	Yes	Yes	Yes	Yes
5–10 years (special permits)	Yes	Yes	Yes	Yes	Yes	Yes	Yes
10 year + (permanent)	Yes	Yes	Yes	Yes	Yes	Yes	Yes
EEC Workers in France and Germany	Yes	Yes	Yes	Yes	Yes	Yes	Yes

[a]Except for Spanish workers.
[b]Except for Algerians since 1977.
[c]Some exceptions made.

Free from Job Restrictions	Free to Change Job and Employer	Free from Geographical Restrictions	May Seek Work without Prior Authorization	Permit Grants Holder Status as Indigenous	Pensions
No	No	Can move if authorized	No	No	Yes
No	No	No	No	No	Yes
No	Yes	No	Yes	No	Yes
Yes	Yes	Yes	Yes	Yes	Yes
No	No	No	No	No	Yes
No	No	No	Yes	No	Yes
No	No	No	Yes	No	Yes
No	Yes	No	Yes	No	Yes
No	Yes	No	Yes	Yes	Yes
No	No	No	No	No	Yes
No	Yes	Usually	Yes	No	Yes
No	Yes	Yes	Yes	Yes	Yes
Yes	Yes	Yes	Yes	Yes	Yes
Yes	Yes	Yes	Yes	Yes	Yes

Appendix J:
Summary of
Sociopolitical Rights

Appendix J

	Associations	General Political Restrictions	Consular Voting Rights	Join Political Parties	Local Government	Regional	National
France	Authorization by minister of the interior necessary when more than one-quarter of all members are foreign and/or officers foreign Free to join French associations with less than one-quarter foreigners; need no authorization	Foreigners must maintain political neutrality	Yes	Tolerated	Extramunicipal consultative boards with appointed foreign delegates	Regional advisory groups without set foreign-worker presentation	Indirect representation through trade unions on advisory councils of governmental bodies specifically concerned with migration policy
Switzerland	Full liberty of association	Foreigners must not disrupt public order or disturb Swiss foreign relations	No	Yes	Appointed delegates to contact centers	Cantonal and regional contact centers with appointed delegates	Foreign representatives (associational leaders) consulted by Federal Commission for the Foreigner Question and representatives on Federal Commission are aliens.
Germany	Full liberty but authorities can require associations composed of a majority of foreigners to register with police	Foreigners must not disrupt public order	Yes	Yes	Appointed delegates to coordination councils throughout the country Locally elected parliaments	State coordinator councils and advisory boards with appointed delegates	Foreign-worker representatives consulted by national advisory commission

	Toleration of Nonviolent Homeland-Oriented Political Activity	Freedom of Expression and Assembly (Includes Press)	Union Membership and Factory Elections	Protest Marches and Demonstrations Require Police Authorization	Homeland Candidates Can Campaign for Votes	Deportations of Foreign Political Activists
France	Yes	Yes[a]	Yes	Yes	Yes	Infrequent
Switzerland	Yes	Yes	Yes	Yes	Yes	Rare
Germany	Yes	Yes	Yes	Yes	Yes	Rare

Index

About the Authors

Mark J. Miller became interested in foreign workers as a student in Aix-en-Provence, France, in 1970-1971. He subsequently worked on a construction crew with migrant workers in Southern France before returning to the Ecole des Hautes Etudes en Sciences Sociales for dissertation research on foreign labor in 1975-1976. He received the Ph.D. in political science at the University of Wisconsin at Madison in 1978, and then joined the faculty of the University of Delaware. In addition to teaching, Dr. Miller has since served as a consultant on foreign workers to the Interagency Task Force on Immigration Policy and the U.S. Department of Labor.

Philip L. Martin developed an interest in migrant workers as a Fulbright Fellow in Germany in 1973-1974. He returned to the University of Wisconsin at Madison and received the Ph.D. in labor economics in 1975. During 1978-1979 he was a Fellow at the Brookings Institution in Washington, D.C., and wrote *Guestworker Programs: Lessons from Europe* (1980). Dr. Martin was senior economist for the Select Commission on Immigration and Refugee Policy in 1979. He is now an associate professor of agricultural economics at the University of California at Davis.